Forsooth he cometh to you with a tale, which holdeth children from play, and old men from the chimney-corner, and pretending no more, doth intend the winning of the mind from wickedness to virtue even as the child is often brought to take most wholesome things by hiding them in such other as have a pleasant taste.

— From *Defence of Poesie* by Sir Philip Sydney

The cartoons, drawn by Jeanette Perkins Brown, first appeared in "Child Guidance," published by the Methodist Publishing House, and in "Children's Religion," published by The Pilgrim Press. They are included in this book through the courtesy of the publishers.

The STORYTELLER
IN RELIGIOUS EDUCATION

How to Tell Stories
to Children and Young People

JEANETTE PERKINS BROWN

A Co-operative Book Published for the
Co-operative Publication Association

THE PILGRIM PRESS · BOSTON

This is one of a series of books produced for interdenominational use by the Protestant denominations working through the Co-operative Publication Association.

PRINTED IN THE UNITED STATES OF AMERICA

We Are All Alike "That Way"

THE TEACHER began her story. The squirming mass of seven-year-olds, whose only acknowledgment of the visitor's presence had been to enlarge the circle with a noisy scraping of chairs, gradually quieted down. As they had been one in cheerful confusion, they now became one in quiet expectancy. As the story progressed, all eyes were on the teacher, whose words held them motionless until the story ended.

"Now, children," the teacher addressed her class — but the spell was broken. Self-consciousness was returning. The children became aware of life as it is, of the visitor, of each other, with a tentative nudging, a tipped-up chair. The teacher raised her voice. "What lesson do we learn from the story?" she probed. Receiving no answer but giggles and hoots as the tipped chair spilled its occupant, she tried again.

"Children," she persisted, "this is the thought I want you to take away with you," but all thoughts had flown by now. There was only action.

The teacher turned to the visitor. "That's the way it always is," she despaired. "They'll listen all right through a story, and then the minute I try to *teach* them something, and give them some one thought to carry home, they're off like that!"

The visitor hedged. "After all, they're much like us adults," she reasoned. "Don't you sometimes find your mind wandering during a sermon or a lecture? I know I do. But if a story is introduced as an illustration, I'm alert and attentive as anything. Then, when the story is over and the sermon or lecture goes on, I may lose interest again."

The teacher stared at her visitor. Here was a coincidence! "You know," she confided wonderingly, "I'm just like you that way."

We are all alike "that way." Rarely is a person found, child or adult, who will not listen to a story. (And rare indeed is the person, child or adult, who appreciates the belaboring of a point made in a story.)

Because the story has an appeal which is universal, and has no age limits, it has been used by sages, prophets, and teachers through the ages to pass on the great historical traditions and religious insights of a people, to stretch imagination, to awaken conscience, to spur to action, to give joy and reflect beauty, to point up a truth by dramatizing it.

"Why do you speak to them in parables?" the disciples asked Jesus.

"The truths can be understood by you," Jesus answered in effect, "whose eyes and ears have been sharpened, but seeing they see not, they have closed their eyes; hearing they hear not, their ears are dull of hearing."

There was a king who had grievously sinned. But his sin did not disturb him. Only when he heard a story were his eyes opened to see and his ears sharpened to hear:

There were two men in one town, a rich man and a poor man. The rich man had many sheep and cattle; the poor man had nothing but a single ewe lamb which he had bought; he fed it, and it grew up with him and his children, it used to eat his own morsels and drink from his cup and nestle in his bosom, just like a daughter. Now a traveller came to visit the rich man, and the rich man spared his own sheep and cattle when he had to make provision for the traveller who had come to visit him; he took the poor man's lamb and prepared that for his visitor.[1]

Righteous anger filled the listener. Furiously he indicted the man whose ruthlessness was so desolating. We can almost hear him shout, "That man deserves to die!" We can almost see him cringe as the storytelling prophet points his finger accusingly and declares, "You yourself are that man!" And the accused,

[1] 2 Samuel 12: 1-4. From *The Bible: A New Translation* by James Moffatt. Copyright 1935 by Harper & Brothers. Used by permission.

whose eyes are opened at last, sees himself as the man who has sinned.

The teaching power of the story has been recognized from primitive times, when it was the only form of literature and the storyteller the only medium for keeping alive events and characters of significance, to the present day, when books like *Gentleman's Agreement* and *Cry, the Beloved Country* stab awake the consciences of a literate but unaware people.

It is not surprising, therefore, that storytelling has been recognized through the ages as an art meriting the skill and mastery which art has always demanded of the artist.

To help those who would be artist-teachers in religious education to know what a story really is, and what it can do, to recognize its relation to other forms of teaching, and (especially) to make the study and practice of storytelling the delightful venture it is, — these are the purposes of this book.

J. P. B.

CONTENTS

CHAPTER I

Why We Need To Be Good Storytellers

The Story Is an Important Educational Tool

There is power in a well-told story, and its qualities are diverse. If it were only for its pure *entertainment value*, its ability to gain and hold attention, we should cherish it.

" Why," a teacher asked her class, " do you think the minister told us the story of the imprint of the dog's paw in the cement floor? " " Well," offered Jimmy, " it kept us quiet! " If the educator considers this a low-level value, he must at least concede its validity.

Because it has this attention-holding power, the story is the shortest and often the most effective way of *driving home a point*. Of one of the most popular preachers of our times it is said, " He is a master of the use of illustration," and those who have attended his classes or listened to his voice over the radio retain the truths he has preached through the vivid pictures his stories have impressed upon their memory.

It can *relieve tensions*, in class, on the playground, at home. Mary Gould Davis, supervisor of storytelling in the New York Public Library for years, tells of the call of distress which came into the library early in the 1940's. Refugee children from Austria and Germany, all of whom had been through tragic experiences before their escape to the United States, were cared for during the day by Trude Frankl, herself a refugee social worker from Vienna. But nothing Miss Frankl could do could make those children forget themselves or their past. Huddled in a scared little group in the gymnasium of a church which offered them shelter, they did not talk, much less play. In despair she called the Public Library to ask for a storyteller to try to break this horrid spell. Miss Davis herself answered the challenge, but tremblingly. What would be the right stories for these small victims of Hitler? Would they listen to her? Would they be frightened by her, as they were by everyone and everything? Would they even understand English?

As the storyteller looked into the circle of white faces with their haunting eyes, the questions were still in her mind. She chose the simplest kind of tale with much repetition in it. The children's eyes never wavered from her face, nor was there any change of expression. But when she had finished, a six-year-old boy who seemed to be a kind of leader of the group rose, put his heels together, pointed his finger at her, and announced, "You-will-say-all-again!" And she, who well knew there is no greater tribute to the power of the story than a child's "Tell it again," knew now that barriers had fallen and child souls were being released.

Many a tense situation in our own church-school classes has been eased and forgotten with the hearing of a story, so that creative group work, impossible before, could be carried on. And every storytelling mother knows its persuasive power to temper emotions and check incipient rebellions.

American Indian parents know its value. Abrupt commands to "Do this" or "Stop that" are not given. Without the aid of child study classes, they know a recipe for correcting tendencies, nipping resentments in the bud, and warding off the "I won't's" or "Why do I have to's." They give the reason for the desired behavior in the form of a story in which the suggested action is portrayed, with the good or evil consequences to the doer, or the shirker.

The story can *effect a happy relationship between the story-teller and listener*. The storytelling parent or teacher here too knows her advantage. There is a special rapport which results from the enjoyment together of a venture into storyland. Shared wonder, shared thrills, shared insights produce an association that is precious.

> You may have tangible wealth untold,
> Caskets of jewels and coffers of gold.
> Richer than I you could never be;
> I knew someone who told stories to me.[1]

The story can *develop the imagination and cultivate a sense of humor*. It enables the listener to look beyond things as they are and see things as they might be. He even sees himself in a role beyond himself, engaged in tasks beyond his present powers. No architect ever designed a cathedral without the picture in his imagination of a building that never had been erected. No builders of a better world can bring it to pass without first imagining what it would be like. Imagination is the first component of faith in the Unseen.

A sense of humor is as important as imagination in the development of a religious personality. Marie Shedlock, in her valuable book, *The Art of the Story-Teller*,[2] quotes Thackeray in saying, ". . . if humor only meant laughter, but the humorist professes to awaken and direct your love, your pity, your kindness, your scorn for untruth and pretensions, your tenderness for the weak, the poor, the oppressed, the unhappy."

The Christian would say that these are Christian virtues and is grateful for any method which cultivates them. Added powers are given the story with the introduction of humor; imagination helps the listener to a sense of proportion. It shows him, to quote Miss Shedlock again, " his real position in the universe, and prevents an exaggerated idea of his own importance. It develops the logical faculty, and prevents hasty conclusions. It brings about a clearer perception of all situations,

---

[1] From a pamphlet, *Youth and Story Telling*, by Cynthia Pearl Maus. Copyright 1928 by the International Council of Religious Education, Chicago, Ill. Used with permission.

[2] From *The Art of the Story-Teller* by Marie L. Shedlock. Appleton-Century-Crofts, Inc. Used by permission of Curtis Brown, Ltd.

enabling the child to get the point of view of another person. It is the first instilling of philosophy into the mind of a child and prevents much suffering later on when the blows of life fall upon him."

Who is not grateful for the story of the cock who thought his crowing ushered in the dawn, or such favorites as " Epaminondas " and " To Your Good Health " (see Appendix), and the humor of that whimsical collection, *Story-tell Lib?*

The story can inform and enlighten; it can clarify vision and help to solve problems. It can change attitudes. It can set a standard for behavior. It can give new insights; new appreciations come, new resolves. It can " feed and quicken the spirit," lead to worship, and stir to action.

We have seen many values that the story may have in religious education and could mention more. But in all the listing which value makes the most impression? Which can you remember best, one of those enumerated in the last paragraph, or, say, the one shown in the story's ability to relieve tensions? Which is the most convincing? Do you even believe all the claims made in the paragraph above? But is there any doubt in your mind about a story's power to release the pent-up frightened spirit of a child?

We may know, intellectually, many facts about the universe. But for all our knowledge we may not be moved to the wonder and gratitude for its dependable laws that Alice Geer Kelsey's story, " The Constant Star," may arouse in us, through our anxiety and final relief shared with her hero. (See Appendix.)

We may be able to rattle off impressive statistics about the millions of displaced persons wandering over the earth. But all the statistics in all the reports have not the pull on our heartstrings or our purses contained in a well-told story of one homeless, friendless child, with a name and a specific experience.

We may know quite well what our duties are towards our fellow man, just as that lawyer probably did who invited the parable of the good Samaritan. But a story in which we can identify ourselves in a living way with the characters makes us see and *feel* the effects of certain types of behavior on persons like ourselves. It is the element of feeling in the well-told story which makes all the difference. There are no feelings in facts, in lists, in statistics.

That is why the story is an invaluable tool in an educational area, in which the creation of attitudes and relationships is more important than facts. And that is why it behooves those of us who are teachers, or leaders of worship, or directors of religious education, or writers of courses of study, or preachers, or parents, or friends of children to know what makes a good story and when and how to tell it.

THE PLACE OF THE STORY IN THE CURRICULUM

At the beginning of the century the obligation to learn how to use this tool effectively was recognized, and textbooks to develop skill in the art of storytelling were eagerly studied. The most prized teachers were the expert storytellers. Our " lesson books " gave first place in importance to the story, unfortunately sometimes to the exclusion of other aids to teaching. A story was provided for every Sunday and became the core of the teaching session. Many teachers came to think of the " lesson " in terms of preparing for the story, telling the story and expressing the story.

WEAKNESSES IN OVERDEPENDENCE ON THE STORY

The weaknesses in using storytelling as the only method of teaching are obvious. It may become an end in itself instead of a means to an end. There are many roads to learning, the chief one being first-hand experience. The story, used exclusively, becomes a substitute for experience, or second-hand experience. Emotions are aroused for which no outlet in action is provided. Characters can be made so vivid that the listener, completely identifying himself with the hero, not only toils and suffers with him vicariously, but, also vicariously, enjoys the unearned emotional satisfaction of the hero's earned reward. Thus he feels no need for real effort on his part to achieve such satisfaction.

Moreover this overuse of the story, besides making the teaching monotonous, meant the neglect of methods which might be used more effectively.

New Emphasis on Learning Through Activity

When the great educators of the day made us aware of the limitations of "transmissive education" and teachers began to see the significance of such slogans as "we learn by doing," "the child acts it out before he takes it in," activity took the important place in the curriculum and the learning of new skills occupied the interests of student teachers.

The "project method" or "activity curriculum" embraced many methods in one. Trips and discussions, building and painting filled the day-school sessions. Storytelling in training courses was relegated to a minor place, if included at all.

This was so also in religious education. While our courses still carried a story for nearly every Sunday, other methods were suggested to help children grow religiously — through experiences with materials, with nature, with people, and through their own creative activities. The more experienced teachers made use of many methods, placing less and less importance on perfecting themselves in the practice of storytelling until we have grown out of the habit of seriously studying this art. This is our loss, for there is always need of the joy and beauty and inspiration that a good story, well told, can bring, and there are many ways of using it in good teaching procedures.

NEW USES FOR THE STORY

A story can never take the place of experience, but it can *prepare a group for an experience*, so that the experience itself will be entered into with expectancy and intelligence. A visit in the fall to a Jewish neighbor's Succoth booth, for instance, preceded by as much of the Bible story [3] of its origin as is suitable to your age group, makes the dramatic story come alive for them. Children thrill to a realization of its long history. "And they're still doing it! " was a third grade boy's wondering comment at his first visit to one.

A story can *interpret an experience* for which there has not been such preparation, pointing it up, making it significant; or can enrich it by adding to one originally told.

Further stories from Nehemiah, for example, give the Succoth experience additional meaning,[4] as the children hear what happened when the desert wanderings were over, and the

---

[3] Exod. 15: 22; Lev. 23: 33-44; Deut. 16: 13-17.
[4] Neh. 8: 14-18.

people settled in the Promised Land, grew prosperous, forgot the old laws, lost their lands to conquerors, and finally, a forlorn remnant, with city walls and temple in ruins, welcomed and helped Nehemiah in rebuilding; gathered in the open place to hear the reading of the old forgotten laws, and heard among them the one pertaining to the Feast of the Tabernacles, and the reminder of the leafy booths. One, two, or three stories are here, but each deserves the attention to the rules for good storytelling which succeeding chapters will suggest.

A story may *start a project* or, in the midst of one, give new zest and purposefulness in work on it. Such a story as " The Little Boy with a Big Stick," based on true incidents (see Appendix), gives the reason for a neighborhood center. Children not only see a center function but recognize its worth, because they are interested in a little boy whose feelings would be like their own.

Often a story, listened to for its pure entertainment value, is seized upon for its *dramatic possibilities.* " Let's act it out " may lead to sharing the dramatization with another group, and all the experiences which accompany " giving a play."

A dramatization may become a project in itself, or it may be part of a larger one. In an extensive project there are numerous opportunities for other kinds of stories, as different needs arise. Informal activities often produce problems in working together. Sometimes the teacher knows just the story which will suggest a solution. Undesirable attitudes towards persons or groups, or towards certain phases of life, emerge in spontaneous conversation which, through a well-chosen story, may be directed into more wholesome channels. See " Nathan's Friend," " That Novo," and " The Little Boy with a Big Stick " in the Appendix.

Sometimes to give *background for discussion and planning,* fresh information is needed which a story may supply, though the main purpose of a story is never to provide information.

A story can *lift an everyday experience to a higher plane*, creating a mood which brings about unplanned worship in the class. Told in the service of worship, listeners see themselves in new relationships, and new values in their undertaking emerge.

Increased importance is given their project and new enjoyment of it may result. Stories (well told) from the mission field or war-devastated areas, gleaned from church magazines, news reports, or publications of such organizations as the American Friends Service Committee, have greatly increased enthusiasm for class enterprises in world friendship. See " Janek's Problem " and "Anna and the Speckled Hen " in the Appendix.

A project may develop around the study of a great scientist, humanitarian, artist, or teacher, whose life and talents have been dedicated to the benefit of mankind. A series of continued stories will make the personality increasingly real, bringing with them new appreciations, if each story is a *story*, and not merely a series of disconnected events or statements about the person.

This leads us to the consideration of what a story really is — and another chapter.

Suggested Assignments

1. Summarize on paper the points made under " The Story Is an Important Educational Tool," then those under " New Uses for the Story," and check those for which you can bring an illustration.

2. Show how a story could prepare your class for a trip around the church or to an institution in the neighborhood. What kind of story would you choose? What kind might enrich the experience later?

3. What story in your reading has made a deep impression on you?

4. Recall a story which has impressed you in a lecture or sermon. How much of the lecture or sermon do you recall?

CHAPTER II

The Story and Its Parts

DEFINITION OF A STORY

Before we can become good storytellers we must know what a good story is, and how to distinguish it from an inferior one. The claims made for it in Chapter I are great. How can a story be so presented in our teaching as to move the listener emotionally? How does it gain its effect? What makes it a work of art?

We know it is narration, but evidently more than a mere presentation of facts or events, something other than a vehicle for information or description or exhortation. What is this "plus"?

Let us consider a definition by Edward Porter St. John, a master of the art of storytelling. He describes a story as "a narrative of true or imaginary events which form a vitally related whole, so presented as to make its appeal chiefly to the emotions rather than to the intellect." [1] Much is packed into that definition. Whole suggests unity; one consistent line of thought, one purpose; one set of events, each important to the others and to the outcome; one kind of feeling aroused. We recall the classic folk tales, "Cinderella," for example, or the brief allegories of Laura E. Richards (see Appendix), or the parables of Jesus, as perfect examples of such unity.

Moreover, as it is one "whole" that each story is striving for, we shall find that each is told from one point of view. It

---

[1] From *Stories and Story Telling* by Edward Porter St. John. The Pilgrim Press. Used by permission.

may be that of the spectator or the narrator, who sees only what happens and relates the events objectively. Or it may be that of one of the characters in the story, whose thoughts and emotions are revealed as the plot unfolds. But a story which jumps from one point of view to another, trying to get inside the minds of all the characters, is confusing and inartistic. We shall come back to this point later, with illustrations.

THE STORY FORM

The narrative which is a " unified whole " gains its effectiveness through no accident. Consider the parables or the old folk tales mentioned above. You will see that they follow a pattern. They are put together after a certain fashion.

There is (1) a brief *Introductory Setting* for the events to follow, for example:

Once upon a time there was a girl whose mother died and whose father married for his second wife the proudest and unkindest woman that ever was seen.

There was once a child who was untidy.[2]

A certain man was going down from Jerusalem to Jericho.

(2) There is *Action* in which event follows event in logical sequence (this is the body of the story); (3) a *Climax* towards which every event has moved; and (4) a brief *Conclusion* which leaves no loose ends, no questions.

As soon as one realizes that there is a story form, that story writing and storytelling are not a haphazard relating of incidents, but have definite factors that can be recognized and mastered, the making of stories becomes a fascinating practice. Preparation for telling a story becomes an exercise of reading the story, making note of its high points, and filling in the details.

[2] From " The Pig Brother," in *The Golden Windows*, Laura E. Richards. Copyright 1903 by Little, Brown & Co.

WHEN A STORY **IS NOT** A STORY

A STORY is NOT a report.

A STORY is NOT a series of descriptions, scenic or otherwise, colorful though they may be, and transporting the story-teller to realms of ecstasy.

WHEN A STORY **IS NOT** A STORY

Children instinctively grasp the four steps in a good story. Second-grade children were once asked for ideas for a picture storybook. " It has to begin," one said, " and then " — making a quick gesture through the air — " it has to go right along. And something has to happen, and then it has to stop."

" But this story has to be about a trip," the teacher explained. " What would a travel story be like? "

" Well," they considered, " something has to make the family go on a trip " (recognition of introductory step). " Then they go and things happen on the way " (action). " Then they come home and something has to have happened " (climax). "And that's the end " (conclusion).

Each step of the four has such a definite function it is important enough to devote a chapter to it. But the most important step of all, around which the whole story creation moves, is the climax, the point of the story. Without a point there is no story. Each of the other steps leads to it. Focusing of all action and description on this outcome contributes to that necessary " unity " in a story, that " vitally related whole."

In telling a story, then, if the climax is kept in one's mind, the effect will not be dissipated by the introduction of irrelevant details, or blurred by the storyteller's vague notion of what the story is all about. Rather it will of itself suggest a pertinent beginning, determine the direction of the action, and indicate a suitable conclusion.

THE RULES APPLY TO DIFFERENT KINDS OF STORIES

There are different types of stories, but they all follow the general pattern.

(a) *The Plot Story*. A hero is involved in a situation where the final outcome is uncertain. It is the outcome which makes the climax. The storyteller knows that climax, and keeps it in mind from the beginning sentences, designed to rouse interest in both hero and outcome; through events which follow, which help the hero along or obstruct him; to the final act, which breaks down the last barrier and concludes the story. Every boy and girl who listens to the story of Joseph recognizes this as a " plot " story.

(b) *The Problem Story*. The hero has a problem whose solution is the climax. The introduction must indicate the problem and sufficiently engage the listener's interest to make him want the hero to find the answer. He will enter with the hero into each event that follows, hoping to find the solution; welcome it when it comes as the climax, and settle back, contented, with the concluding sentence. The story of Jesus' answer to the lawyer's question, " Who is my neighbor? " is a familiar example.

(c) *The Quest* has a slightly different slant, but the function of each step is similar to that of the problem story. The climax of the search comes at the point when the hero finds what he is seeking. The introduction makes the outcome exceedingly desirable but difficult. Each act in the sequence of events may seem to make his goal unattainable, but actually brings it nearer. " The Quest of the Holy Grail " comes immediately to mind as one illustration.

(d) *The Journey* is, in a way, another quest, but works towards the climax of the journey's end. The introduction in a well-told story of a journey compels interest in the one who is journeying, and the reason for his setting forth. Each step leads to a milestone or hinders progress towards it. Arrival, in a strong climax, is attended by relief, if the suspense has been well kept.

(e) *The Character Story*. Some stories deal with character development or change. But character growth is a slow process. A short story which is a unit can deal only with a single experience or set of experiences within a brief time span. One experience cannot be expected to change character, but it may definitely affect attitudes, from which character is formed. Attitudes are the result of feelings which one has about what has happened to him. A " character growth " story, then, would be one in which the hero's feelings are so affected that a change in attitude (and consequent acts) takes place, which may eventually transform or establish character. In such a story the introduction would show the " hero " at one stage in his life, and more or less in need of change, but appealing enough for listeners to care what happens to him. The climax is the turning point towards which all action has been possible, though not inevitable. Zacchaeus furnishes an example of this type of story.[3]

JOKES AND EPISODES

Anyone who has ever told a joke knows that it is the point that makes it funny. If we don't see the point, it isn't funny. If there is no point, there is no joke. A good storyteller will make even the relating of a walk down the street entertaining by building up to a climax which is more or less a surprise. Examples of this kind of episode or anecdotal reporting are found under such titles as " Life in These United States " in *The Reader's Digest*, or " Life's Like That " in the British edition. One has only to try writing up a personal experience, or something amusing which has happened to a friend, to realize that the surprise ending does not just happen. It is only achieved by building up to a climax.

---

[3] See also biographical treatment, chapters III and IX.

This very building up to a climax brings us back to the story form and the four elements of which it is composed, Introduction, or Beginning; Sequence of Events, or Action; Climax, and Conclusion. Each step has its special importance.

Why Beginnings Are Important

The beginning must capture the interest of the listener at once. The script writer for radio knows that this has to be accomplished in the first few seconds. If it is not, dials click before many have passed, and the listener is gone. The story-teller on the platform or in the circle may not lose his listeners physically, but he can lose their attention and good will by a long or dull beginning, or one which seems to lead nowhere.

The beginning, though not longer than a sentence or two in a short story, must introduce the leading character, put him in the proper setting, and awaken curiosity about his problem or situation. It must give a clue to what the story is about. It anticipates, without predicting, the end. It suggests the problem which the climax will resolve. Note the types of expectancy that these beginnings arouse:

A sower went forth to sow.

Once the North Wind and the Sun had a quarrel about which was stronger.

There was once a princess named Marigold who had never seen the light of day.

Long ago, in a small country village in England, there lived a boy named Dick Whittington. Dick's father and mother had died, and the boy had a hard time getting along by himself.

If anybody had told Gilberto when he awakened that morning all that would happen before he went to bed that night he never would have believed it.

Jesus was a hunted man. His enemies were plotting his arrest. King Herod was on his trail. (From a story told by Elsie Spriggs.)

The beginning can also give the flavor of the story to come, — the classical, the fanciful, or humorous one can be recognized at once, for example:

In the days when good King Arthur ruled the land. . . .

In olden times, when the angels walked the earth in the form of men. . . .

Long ago there lived a king who was such a mighty monarch that whenever he sneezed everyone in the whole country had to say, " To your good health! "[4]

Now it came to pass in the days when the Judges ruled, that there was a famine in the land of Judah.

Of course you know that dragons were once as common as motor omnibuses are now, and almost as dangerous.[5]

It was the evening of the day set for Queen Elizabeth's visit to Kenilworth.

Pushmi-pullyus are now extinct. That means, there aren't any more. But long ago, when Doctor Dolittle was alive, there were some of them still left in the deepest jungles of Africa; and even then they were very, very scarce.[6]

The shorter the introductory step is, the better, provided it establishes interest in the character or the plot. Descriptions will not do this. Long explanations within the story tend to dissipate rather than arouse curiosity. The missionary who wants the good will and co-operation of his audience best gains it by plunging into a story in which his listeners identify themselves at once with the people he is trying to help. Note the

---

[4] From " To Your Good Health " in *Crimson Fairy Book*, edited by Andrew Lang. Longmans, Green and Co.

[5] From " The Last of the Dragons," by E. Nesbit in *Five of Us and Madeline*. Greenberg Pub. Co., Inc. Used by permission.

[6] From " The Rarest Animal of All," by Hugh Lofting in *The Story of Dr. Dolittle*. J. B. Lippincott Co. Used by permission.

difference between the two approaches shown in the first and
the two following illustrations:

Our missionary work among the Indians was started in 1887. Since then
hundreds of Indian boys who wanted an education have been helped.
Last year's graduating class numbered eighty-one. The work has grown
so that we badly need a new building to increase our dormitory capacity.
Without it, many Indians will be disappointed;

and

Big Chief Flying Hawk sat on his horse looking down at his son;

or

Young Swift-as-Lightning ran to meet his father. It had been three days
since Chief Flying Hawk had left the reservation on his important errand.
"What did you find?" the boy called as he came within shouting distance.
"What did they say?"

The first beginning lulls one to sleep. The speaker has
already lost his advantage. He has given us no picture, he has
not even roused hope of one. Each of the others presents a
picture and a promise. Whatever facts are forthcoming here,
they will be personalized and dramatized, making the "appeal
to the emotions rather than to the intellect."

Beginnings to Avoid. There is the beginning which tells too
much, revealing the climax instead of arousing curiosity about it.

This story is about a boy who was so brave he got a prize for helping a
great many children who might have been hurt when a sandbank began
to fall;

or

I'm going to tell you about a shepherd boy named David who killed a
wicked giant with his slingshot.

The storyteller has already given away his climax; there is no
surprise in store, no need, really, to go on listening.

Then there is the vague beginning, which gives such a blurred
picture that no clear impression at all is gained, and interest is
consequently lost.

This story happened a long time ago — well, not too long ago, but not just lately. There was this boy, I've forgotten his name, but let's call him John or Bill. He lived in some city — I don't recall whether it was Chicago or New York; oh, no, it was San Francisco. I remember thinking when I heard it that it *wasn't* the city near the place where they make the moving pictures.

By this time, of course, it matters not to the listener where the city was, or what happened to the boy, — or was it a girl?

Another beginning which is mistakenly supposed to be effective is the one which begins with a parent or teacher telling a story to a child. This story-within-a-story is seldom as gripping as a story directly attacked, and to children is confusing.

Jerry had had a hard day. Everything had gone wrong. He had fallen and hurt his knee when he was teasing his sister, chasing her around the orchard. He had lost the lucky penny Uncle John had given him last summer. More than usual he looked forward to the story his mother would tell him before he went to bed.

"Once upon a time," she began, as they settled themselves comfortably, "there was a boy named David. . . ."

The storyteller has invited the listener to identify himself with a boy named Jerry and his troubles. Now she switches the invitation to a boy named David. Whose fortunes is the listener to follow? If David's, then why not begin with him, and trust the story to carry its message alone?

SEQUENCE OF EVENTS

Action and suspense are the characteristics of the second part of the story.

Action. To quote Dr. St. John again, " The sequence of events presents the movement of the story toward the climax which gives meaning to the whole. The great essential is that it shall be orderly, presenting the necessary facts step by step, and preparing for the climax without revealing it in advance." Note how the story of the traveler on his way from Jerusalem to Jericho progresses in " orderly " fashion, presenting the " necessary facts step by step."

1. He goes down from Jerusalem.
2. He falls among thieves who strip and beat him, leaving him half-dead.
3. The priest arrives, passes him by.
4. The Levite arrives, passes him by.
5. The Samaritan arrives:
    is moved with compassion,
    attends his wounds,
    sets him on the beast,
    takes him to the inn and cares for him, even paying in advance for continued care.

Suspense. The element of suspense, which keeps the outcome hanging in the balance, is what provides the dramatic quality in a story. The greater the suspense the more rapt the attention, the more impressive the point, and the greater the real satisfaction and relief at the climax. We pay too little attention to this in stories told in the church school, which gives our storytelling a reputation for tameness. " It's a nice little Sunday-school story," alas, means one with little dramatic tension.

If progress is too easy, if there is no conflict, no struggle, if no choices are presented to make the outcome uncertain, we

DON'T'S FOR STORY ENDINGS

have only narrative instead of plot, not a story in the sense in which we are using the term.

Folk tales which have been told and retold for centuries usually fall naturally into the story form referred to and follow the pattern. In fact, they helped to set the pattern. It is worth while to study them, to analyze their parts, and observe how they become a "related whole." Recall the rapid action in "Cinderella," for instance, or "Red Riding Hood," or "The Three Bears." Note how event follows event, always mounting to a climax, but with enough hazards in their course to keep the listener or reader in doubt as to how the story will come out.

The Climax. We have already considered the importance of the climax, and know that if it is weak, the story is weak. It is the high point; it carries the real message or moral of the story. If this is not apparent in the climax, or if there is no climax, the story is a poor story or has been poorly told. And nothing can be done about it, for we have come to the end — or almost the end.

The Ending. All that remains is to cut the plot thread which has been unwinding. The story has been told. Questions raised at first have been answered, and it is time to stop. There is an abrupt drop from the high point the mounting action has reached. The temptation to go on and on after there is nothing more to say, to point up the moral, or to begin to "teach," as the lady quoted in the book's Introduction would call it, must be quashed. Only a sentence or two will be needed to leave the mind at rest, able to go back over the story at will, and find again its deeper meaning.

Then the Prince and Sleeping Beauty were married with all splendor, and they lived happily all their lives.

And to this day no giant has ever been seen there.

After this Aladdin and his wife lived in peace. When the Sultan died, Aladdin ascended the throne, and ruled for many years.

DO'S FOR STORY ENDINGS

LEAVE ALL CHARACTERS ACCOUNTED FOR—

—Even if you must resort to the child story-teller's solution, i.e., "And one day when they were walking down to the front gate, they all died." E.P. St. John.

STOP WHEN YOU'RE THROUGH

Beginning Development Climax Conclusion

GO GO GO STOP

STORY
PROBLEM
PLOT
QUEST JOURNEY
J.P.B.

The climax is only one step removed from the end. A concluding sentence is usually sufficient. Don't kill interest by explaining, interpreting or moralizing.

"Yes," rustled the mother oak, "you are now an oak tree. This is your real life." And the little oak tree was glad, and stretched higher and higher toward the sun.

And when Jacob heard all that had come to pass, his heart leaped with joy, and he journeyed down into the land of Egypt to abide with Joseph, his son, and with all of his sons, so long as he lived.

A calm radiance of wonder and joy lighted the pale face of Artaban like the first ray of dawn on a snowy mountain-peak. A long breath of relief exhaled gently from his lips. His journey was ended. His treasures were accepted. The Other Wise Man had found the King.[7]

SUGGESTED ASSIGNMENTS

1. Bring to class: (a) A straight newspaper report; (b) A newspaper account which a reporter has made into a story through its emotional appeal.

2. Make a synopsis of a short story you have read, by giving its Introduction, its Sequence of Events, its Climax, and Conclusion.

3. Classify one of the stories in your church-school textbook as to type, i.e., Plot, Problem, Quest, Journey, Character Story.

4. Bring to class one good beginning for a story, and one poor one which you have found.

[7] From "The Other Wise Man," by Henry van Dyke. Used by permission of Harper & Brothers.

CHAPTER III

The Story Form and Children

An understanding of the laws governing any art makes mastery of that art easier, modifications and adaptations in practice more possible. We have put great emphasis on the story form and the importance of each of the four parts of the story. But many stories are published singly, in collections, or in lesson materials, which seem to disregard rules as given here.

Some of these may be beautiful and moving because written by master storytellers. Such masters are familiar enough with the laws for good storytelling to be able to gain their effects through artistry of their own. But most of us are apprentices, learning the rules. We read many stories — may even write some — which "get by" editors and publishers, but which are actually ineffective in the telling. The message may be too obvious. The point may be lost in unimportant details. The story may lack the build-up to make a telling climax. Or perhaps the writer has misjudged the capacities or interests of his audience.

Again, a story to be read may contain many paragraphs of description. The young reader will probably skip these to get on with the action. The author never knows. But the storyteller knows she must get on with the action, or she'll have no audience — so she skips the description anyway. If the storyteller is aware of what makes storytelling effective at a particular age level, she can take the material at hand and herself adapt it to her audience's interests.

Listeners of any age tend to identify themselves with the main character in the story. If they cannot enter sympathetically into his experiences, either because (1) the character does not appeal to them, or (2) the experiences are too foreign to their own, or (3) the presentation is too complicated or too elementary to interest them, or (4) the vocabulary and length are not suited to their age level, even the well-written story loses its power. Let us consider the characteristics and interests of children at different stages in relation to storytelling.

The Nursery Age

This is the "here and now" age. Every mother knows that stories for the two- or three-year-olds are best appreciated when told to the accompaniment of some natural activity — dressing, undressing, bathing, eating — and which have a single character, a recognizable setting, and simple action. The interest span is too brief to attempt storytelling in groups, and while a child may enjoy the picture storybook, his chief interest will be a motor one, of turning the pages. Plot and so-called techniques of storytelling are disregarded at this early age.

Four-Year-Olds

Four-year-olds make better listeners, but still like their stories told to them personally or in very small groups, and in very small quantities. Vocabulary is simple but important, for words are beginning to fascinate them; and emphasis in the story is on action. The story parts begin to take form. Beginnings, continuity, and conclusions are in order.

Four-year-olds can create their own stories, and a study of such original narratives gives insight into what does interest them. One finds nouns and verbs in profusion, but few, if any, adjectives or adverbs. Action is the main element. There are no descriptions. In the following, dictated by a four-year-old, there are 180 words with thirty-three verbs. Thirty-two of the thirty-three are action verbs. This story " goes somewhere! "

A mouse *ran* under the table while the maid wasn't *looking*. Then he *ran* under the Christmas tree, and then he *ran* under the chair. The maid *saw* the mouse and he *ran* away and the poor maid *was* mad. He *ran* to the country, and he *wandered* around the country. He *went* into a house and *climbed* up a shelf and there he *found* some cheese. He *uncovered* the paper and then he *ate* it. He *went* outside and *saw* a little red car and *jumped* into it. Then he *rode* it home. When the maid *saw* him she *laughed* so hard that she *plopped* on the floor. Then she *put* him in a cage. She *fed* him sugar and apples. He *jumped* out of the cage and he *jumped* into a big truck and he *rode* it to the city. He *wandered* around until he *came* to a house and there he *found* some butter. He *took* it home and *attached* it on to the cheese. The maid *jumped* with delight and *fell* plop on the floor again.

Note the ending which, while bringing the story to a humorous conclusion, repeats artistically a striking note in the body of the story. As indicated in the cartoon (page 24) even young children feel the need for a conclusive finish to a story.

One four-year-old ended his story:
"And they ate and ate until they were all finished. And then they got married. And that's the end."

Another, whose story began with:
" Once a dog was exploded by a car because he didn't look each way; he didn't look any way," ended with: " They went to every place that they thought they could fix him up, but they couldn't so they put him in a seminary."

Still another concludes his story of a runaway rabbit:
" He got out of the safe place and lived happily ever after with his family, and they never made things go lost again. And this was a true story."

Teachers who encourage four-to-six-year-olds to create their own stories find the activity rewarding in more than one way. The children's narratives reflect vocabulary and images from stories read or told them, and impressions from their own experiences. More important, the activity is often a means of revealing and releasing inhibitions which are barriers to normal development and happy relationships. A story dictated by another four-year-old, " The Lion in the Church," and what happened afterward, illustrates the therapeutic values in the procedure. The child dictating located his church in France, as far away as possible, but the disguise is thin. His nursery school is in the church tower!

A LION BROKE a window and also he broke all the windows of a tower in a big church in France. He came up by the stair. He came down by the elevator. And he ate up the elevator man. Then he went outside and ate up all the passengers on the avenue where the church was. And then he went up again by the stair and he ate up four teachers on the fourteenth floor of that church. Those teachers were Miss Barnouw, Mrs. Braasch, Mrs. Taylor and Mr. Swan. He ate them up. He ate up all the children. Then the lion tore off the handle from the window. Then he broke off two such bars next to the window. Then he damaged the radiator into such little pieces (demonstrates with fingers). Then he broke a table. Then he damaged the glass on the clock. Then he ate up all the parents at the parents' meeting. And then he went down to the fifth floor and there he broke the window and tore off the handle and the bars and damaged the table and the chairs and windows in the doors. And he ate up all the children on the fifth floor. Then he tore off two ear-rings from both ears of somebody. Then he tweaked them. Then he spanked them and then he gobbled that person all up. Then he damaged the waste-paper basket. Then the shelves where the books are. Then he tore off the dress from a person. He tore off the handle from a door and a door lock. He went into a house. He broke the windows and tore everything into pieces. Then he damaged the radiators and broke up the closets. Then he damaged the toys of a child. Then he broke the dresser and tore the clothes apart. He broke the dresser and the windows of all the apartment. Then he damaged the furniture and the beds, the bookshelf and the bookcase. He tore the books apart. He broke a belt from a father, a boat from a child. He gobbled the child up. Then he damaged two bars of the window. Then he broke all the doors and the piano. Then he drank the milk and broke the cracker to pieces. Then he broke the tools of the father and the tool cabinet. Then he ate up the mother and the father and the child and the whole house. Finally he damaged the tea kettle.

All the people were eaten up. He went into the woods to find a fairy and the fairy was his wife. And she gave him everything to eat that he wanted.

— The Lion in the Church, told by a Four-Year-Old to Elsa Barnouw.

Comments by Miss Barnouw:

The story was told with fiendish glee. All of us laughed heartily during the telling. Corky wanted the lion to be punished for all his dreadful misdeeds, but Bobby refused to accept any such suggestion.

" No-no — nothing happened to him! "

The story gave Bobby tremendous release. Immediately after telling it he climbed to the top of the big jungle gym for the first time this year.

FIVE-YEAR-OLDS

Five-year-olds also need stories with simple images, familiar settings, short sentences, actions in close sequence. They like much direct discourse. Stories can either be true to life or highly imaginative, but not a mixture. Most enjoyed is the cumulative story, with few characters (animals, families). Five-year-olds love rhythmic repetition. " Henny-Penny," " The Old Woman and Her Pig," " The Three Little Pigs," " The Little Red Hen," and " The Gingerbread Man " of nursery lore come to mind as patterns. The story form is followed: the plot interest derives from cumulative effects more than from complications. Suspense is often provided by the simple means of delaying the outcome; e.g., " They looked under the bed; he wasn't there. They looked in the closet. He wasn't there," etc., etc., until finally he *is* where they look, and curiosity is satisfied.

A father we knew kept his young daughter entranced night after night with the wanderings of Nuxie, their dog. Nuxie wanted a bone and went hunting. He went to the library next door, but not a bone was there. He went to the jeweler's, next to the library, but there were no bones there. The storyteller would lead his listener right down the village street, sustaining suspense and cultivating a sense of humor through the absurd visits to the milliner's, the dry-goods store, the bank. Finally they would reach the butcher's, and *there* was a bone! The next night Nuxie would journey up the other side of the street. After visiting the post office, theater, hardware store, church, and school, he would smell a bone through the dirt in a yard, or in a neighbor's kitchen. This serial type of story is always popular.

More Group Listening. There is more group listening with five-year-olds than with younger children, but if some wander off to books or toys, a teacher need not be surprised or discouraged. It is not necessarily because the story or storyteller is weak. These children are individualists, with business of their own to attend to, and interest spans are still brief. So long as there are listeners and the others are taken care of, the teacher continues her story.

YOUNGER PRIMARY AGE

At six group activity and listening are much more possible, and story interests include school and an ever enlarging world. The "true to life" or realistic story is enjoyed at this age, though the fantasy story, recognized as such, is also appreciated.

Animal Interest. According to the editors of a popular magazine for children,[1] animal stories are still the most popular. Thousands of children have so testified in a recent survey, and their comments indicate that it does not much matter whether their stories are factual or imaginative. Mr. Tommy Dorsey ("Two-Arrows"), formerly of the Indian department of the American Museum of Natural History, in preparing a book of animal stories told by parents of his tribe to their small children, compares the natures and reactions of animals to those of people,

[1] *Jack and Jill,* Curtis Publishing Company, Philadelphia, Pa.

and says little children see themselves in the behavior of their animal friends, and learn many lessons from them. Surely the long life of the syndicated animal stories of Thornton Burgess indicates wide audience-interest.

The mechanized life of today, however, may have introduced a trend which we should do well to consider. The story of a young teacher is an illustration. She had been taught that children loved animals, so she began a story:

" Once there were three billy-goats. . . ."

" What's a billy-goat? " interrupted a child.

" Why, you know — an animal — with horns —"

" Uh-huh — and lights? "

Anyone familiar with the " little engine " story knows its appeal to younger primary children. Originally told by Mabel C. Bragg under the title of " The Pony Engine," it has many versions. Watty Piper's book, illustrated by Lois Lenski, bears the title, *The Little Engine That Could*.[2] A favorite version places the journey on the night before Christmas, and makes the engine's puffings sound like words. Let us analyze this story for its effectiveness.

A Primary Story Analyzed

1. *Introduction.* Interest and sympathy are won at once. Any story which begins "It was the night before Christmas" creates immediate good will towards story and storyteller. Then there is the clear problem presented, a critical one from any standpoint. A trainload of Christmas presents for the children in the next town is held up. The engine has broken down. What a situation! There must be *some* solution! (Anticipation of climax)

2. *First Step in Action.* The Engine Man at the roundhouse appeals to the biggest, shiniest engine in the yard, for it is quite a pull over the hill to the next town, and the train has any number of cars (with all the

[2] *The Little Engine That Could*, retold by Watty Piper (from " The Pony Engine," by Mabel C. Bragg. Copyright by George H. Doran & Co.). The Platt & Munk Co., Inc.

Christmas presents for which all those children are waiting). The biggest engine is puffing loudly and boastfully, but all it will answer when the Engine Man appeals to its better nature is a snorting " BEEN out today! BEEN out today! " (First obstacle)

Second Step. The Engine Man turns to the next biggest engine. It, too, is a powerful creation, hissing and steaming like a dragon. The Engine Man repeats his appeal, and the second biggest engine turns him down flatly: " Tsoo-oo tsired! Tsoo-oo tsired! " he sighs heavily. (Second setback)

And all this time the Littlest Engine in the whole engine yard is doing his best to attract the attention of the Engine Man. In excited, hopeful little puffs he keeps begging, " Try me! " and at last is heard. " What? Do you think you could carry that great trainload of gifts over the hill so the children in the next town can have their Christmas presents on time tomorrow morning? " The Engine Man is obviously unconvinced. But the Littlest Engine becomes more excited (as do we, hope reviving) as it changes its tune to, " I think I can! I think I can! "

But we are kept in mounting suspense through the *third long step*, the trip itself. The cheery, hopeful tempo of the first " I think I can " slows down as the slope gets steeper. " I-*think*-I-can; I-THINK-I-can," the wheels' revolutions seem to say. Can the brave Littlest Engine make it? " I-THINK-I-can " — it almost stopped at that last pull. But suddenly something happens.

3. *Climax.* The tune has changed: " I-*thought*-I-could; I-thought-I-could; I-thought-I-could," the engine sings confidently and evenly as it goes down the mountain.

4. We hardly need a *Conclusion*, certainly not more than " So all the children in the next town had their presents on time on Christmas morning," to leave the mind completely at rest.

The story is true to form. Its characters are clear-cut, inviting respect or disapproval by their own actions; a problem is presented in the introduction; each step in the action brings its solution nearer, but keeps the outcome in suspense right up to its peak, when the story, and temperatures, drop at once to normal.

Imitation of the engines' " voices "; direct discourse rather than narration or description; rhythm and repetition, are all marks of the well-told story for primary children.

Learning Through the Emotions. Maud Lindsay's "The Promise," "The Song That Travelled," and "The Jar of Rosemary" from *The Story Teller* are patterns of simplicity and charm which teachers of six- and seven-year-olds, remaking or adapting stories, will also find profitable to analyze, both for form and for emotional content. Children feel with the characters in these stories, and we are bound to remember that it is through our feelings that we learn. "How we feel about a person, our neighbor, the world, determines our acts and regulates our scale of values. How we treat each other, how we meet pleasant and unpleasant situations, depend on what attitudes we have formed through our emotions." One notes how, through the action and speech of the characters themselves, not by moralizing or telling the listener what is good, the Lindsay stories elicit an emotional response to what is wholesome, and beautiful, and true.

How does Miss Lindsay achieve those effects? On what does she depend? On very simple, homely "props." In "The Jar of Rosemary," on a little plant in a cottage window, a favorite toy, the love of a little boy for his mother which, after quite understandable struggles, puts her happiness ahead of his own. In "The Promise," on such familiar, easily entered into loyalties as a "wife and a child and a little brown dog," which of course would make the Harper go to any lengths to keep his promise to "eat his Christmas dinner at his own fireside." In "The Song that Travelled," a king's song is tossed from a palace window to a plowboy with a spotted black and white pig, from the plowboy to a goose girl, who buys a blue ribbon for her hair; to a peddler who sells it to her, to the soldier home from the wars, to a sailor starting on his voyage, to a minstrel on the sailor's ship — and back again to the king, who knows he has made a good song that anybody who is happy can sing.

Can we make our Bible stories as visual as these, remembering the value of simplicity?

It is years since we have told Frances Weld Danielson's story of the first Christmas, as published in the earliest beginners' lessons in any graded series. But her opening sentences, by their very simplicity, created a picture which impressed itself on our memory with such clarity that now, long afterwards, they come back to us. She wrote for beginners, but we used to tell the story, just as she wrote it, to appreciative six- and seven-year-olds.

One day a man and a woman traveled slowly along a road. The man's name was Joseph. The woman was Mary, his wife. Mary rode on a donkey. Joseph walked in front and led the donkey. Joseph and Mary were not the only people traveling that day. There were a great many men and women. Some rode on donkeys. Some rode on camels. Some walked. It was winter and cold, and night was coming on, so they were hurrying to get to the little town of Bethlehem before dark. But Mary was very tired. She could not hurry. And so she and Joseph were left far behind.[3]

OLDER PRIMARY CHILDREN

Dramatic Action and Clear Characterization. Plots become more complicated, stories can be longer and more dramatic as children enter the eight-year level. The survey referred to finds the fairy tale second in popularity (with the stories of real life third). The dramatic element of the folk-fairy tale is part of its appeal. Also the characters are well defined and distinguishable. Some are beautiful and good, others beautiful and bad, but there is never any confusion in the mind of the child where beauty of character lies. Honesty, industry, and kindness are rewarded as the child feels " in his inmost parts " they should be, while treachery, selfishness, and cruelty get their just deserts. There is emotional satisfaction in this.

Traits are symbolized by princesses, knights, dragons, or evil stepmothers, but are not recognized as symbols. To a primary

[3] From *The Little Child and the Heavenly Father,* by F. W. Danielson. Copyright by The Graded Press. Used by permission.

child a person or an object is exactly what it appears to be. He does not see hidden meanings or find parallels in other areas of life. The story of the Lost Sheep or the Lost Coin (Luke 15) will be simply a story of a lost sheep or a lost coin. To try to interpret its symbolism when the story is told is only to confuse the children and spoil the story.

This does not mean that the stories the parables tell or suggest have no interest or value for children. As complete narratives, certain ones like the Good Samaritan and the Forgiving Father (a better title than the Prodigal Son) stand on their own merit, carrying their messages directly. Others, indicated rather than told, suggest expansion into story form with definite appeal. The Lost Sheep (or The Good Shepherd) is one of them. If children are at all familiar with lambs, sheep, and shepherd life, there is an immediate response to the loving care of the shepherd and his sacrifices to protect his sheep. " His dependableness is a good thing to think about." Such stories could be told without mention of Jesus. But these, as well as the nature parables, tell us something about Jesus — what he liked, what he noticed and thought important. The very fact that he noted that the mustard seed had grown into such a tall bush and that birds nested in it is interesting. This parable has often been expanded into a wonder-evoking story of growth in connection with experiences with seeds as in the following: [4]

Once there was a seed that was smaller than all the others. It was smaller than those we planted. It was smaller than those the farmer sowed in his field. If you had seen it you would have thought it was just a little dot, or speck. It was a mustard seed.

A man took the mustard seed and planted it in his garden. There was good soil in his garden with just the right kind of food to give the little mustard seed.

The sun sent its warm rays down through the earth and the rain gave it water to drink. Then, though that seed was so tiny that it was like a speck of the soil itself, something began to happen. There was life inside

[4] " The Mustard Seed " from *Growing in God's World*, by Jeanette Perkins Brown. Copyright 1938. Published by The Graded Press. Used by permission.

that little mustard seed, and a little plant began to grow. It split the covering of the tiny seed and sent out a root and sent up a slender, greenish-white shoot. The root grew bigger and the green stem grew stronger until it pushed itself through the ground. It grew and it grew, until it was as tall as the highest of our seedlings. It grew until it was as tall as the tallest of these plants will ever grow. It grew until it was as tall as a bush. It grew until it was as high as the man's waist and then as high as his shoulder, and then as high as the top of his head. It grew until by stretching his arm a man could just reach the top of it. Then he could not reach its top branches at all, and still it kept on growing. At last it was twice as tall as the man. It was a tree so large, and filled with so many of its own little seeds, that the birds came and settled in its branches. They ate some of the seeds, and they scattered many. Wherever the seeds fell a new plant started until there were many trees instead of one.

And all that came from one tiny mustard seed!

THE JUNIOR AGE

Juniors have a more factual approach to their world. School is introducing them to history, geography, science. Maps, charts and time lines in school are helping them to place historic characters and events in their settings in time and geographical locations.

Fixing Stories in Time and Place. " Time and place and causation are important at this age," declares a junior leader. " The ' once upon a time ' beginning doesn't satisfy. When I tell a story of Tyndall I say he lived at the same time as Columbus. If I tell the children about the Amsterdam Conference in 1948, we have a globe to show the relative positions of Amsterdam and our own city. We get on a ship together (the ship on the big poster our steamship line sent us) and travel for ten days before we even reach Holland, where my story begins. Children like to have their story events *placed*."

We remember a complaint of one who said the Bible stories never seemed real to her. " They were just out in the atmosphere somewhere. I wanted to pin them down where they happened, and never could. In school there were maps in our history books, but in Sunday school Palestine was a sort of imaginary country. " Going down from Jerusalem to Jericho meant going down. I visualized a straight steep hill. The avoidance of the route through Samaria to Jerusalem in favor of the longer one the other side of the Jordan would have meant something, if I could have traced it on the map at the time I heard of a journey from Nazareth to Jerusalem."

Another says, " I thought of Nazareth as on the Sea of Galilee. There was a poem with the line ' In Nazareth of Galilee.' How did I know Galilee was the name of both a province and a lake? " And another, " I always thought the Sea of Galilee to be the size of a minor ocean, at least as big as the Mediterranean. I could have been more at home on it, and in Palestine itself, if I could have pictured the ' Sea ' as the same size as the lake our camp is on, around thirteen miles long, and the whole land of Palestine only the size of Vermont or New Hampshire."

Our stories, then, for this age often need a preparatory period, when time and place may be fixed, settings made clear, unfamiliar customs interpreted, to give the story its full significance. An illustration of such a " setting of the stage " preparatory to telling the story, is found in " Thank Offerings " (see Appendix).

Action and Suspense. The interest span of juniors is longer than that of primary children. Their stories may be longer, provided there is plenty of action and suspense.

Struggle and Conflict. Most effective for this age are those stories where struggle and conflict are present. Opposing forces are sometimes presented through contrasts (as in the story just referred to) rather than by difficulties to be overcome. Without a climax, however, in which one force emerges triumphant over another or in which values become clarified, or an end sought is, after struggle, attained, the story leaves the junior boy or girl in a " So what? " attitude.

The Hero Tale. In the hero tale, to keep the outcome in doubt and heighten the suspense, the storyteller plays up each difficulty which the hero has to face. His efforts to overcome

them make the story and prove his worth. Here we realize the difference between the fairy tale and the hero tale, and their respective appeals. Primary children welcome any influence, within or without, natural or supernatural, which will bring relief, get the hero out of his difficulties and distribute awards and punishments satisfactorily. The hero tale appeals to older boys and girls for the reason that the hero's triumph is his own achievement. He does something to prove that he *is* a hero.

This suggests that the model child has no place as a hero of a tale. He must not always know the right answers, act in the perfect way. That may be the adult's idea of an admirable character, but it is not a child's. Indeed, we know how likely children are to turn against the model picture. How did the person *become* this hero whom you as an adult admire? In what situation did he find himself at first? What was he seeking? How did he learn what he knew, and what were the difficulties in his way? That is what makes the story of a person interesting. Juniors should see the hero in his original setting and know just how favorable or unfavorable it was to the

fulfilling of his need, or the attaining of his quest. They must be sufficiently interested in him to enter sympathetically into his need and experiences. They must recognize the consequences of his decision to act in one way or another. Comparisons and contrasts in the story are helping them to form judgments. If the character achieves success through his struggles, the listener has found his own reasons for admiring or revering the person, and has begun to build up his own standards of action.

Many stories we tell of Jesus leave out this element of strength through struggle, and make Jesus' achievement too easy. Repeated stories of this type emasculate him in his early years and rob him of the admiration given freely to heroes of the radio. A boy's-eye view of a hero is seen in a third grader's response to a really well-told story of Jesus. Apparently Jesus had been recognized as heroic for the first time. " Just like the Lone Ranger! " the boy exclaimed.

Biographical Stories.[5] Stories which are true have a special appeal. For this reason biographical stories of men and women of achievement are popular from the third and fourth grades upward. The listener sees an extension of himself in the hero, or becomes in imagination a contemporary who feels the impact of the hero's personality and way of living. In either event, new possibilities within himself are sensed, and this is a good feeling.

One cannot make a neat, compact story which works up to one dramatic climax by stringing many incidents together and covering a life-span in time. These may produce a general impression of a " good " person, but not a compelling personality with a charge to the listener.

However, as we have said, one can select a single incident which typifies the direction of the hero's life, or one stage in his progress, and build it up, through the steps suggested in our story form, to a dramatic climax. A series of such stories (and boys and girls of junior and junior high school age love a series of tales about the same character) may leave a definite and indelible impression.

Or the impact of both a personality and his message may be felt through the right story built around a single episode or teaching of a master. Chapters VIII and IX will deal more fully with both serials and single teachings. The point we wish to make here is that each episode in a life or each " chapter " in the continued story should have merit of its own as a story.

---

[5] See also comments in Chapter IX on the biographical story.

Suggested Assignments

1. *For everybody.* Think of stories you have enjoyed most at different stages from kindergarten up. Can you analyze their appeal?

2. *For workers with beginners or kindergarten children.* Make up a story around an everyday experience for a five-year-old, according to the suggestions given so far.

3. *For primary leaders.* How could the story of Naaman's little serving maid (2 Kings 5: 1-14), or of Elisha's little room on the roof (2 Kings 4: 8-11, or first part of 13), be told for seven-year-olds, to fit into the patterns of primary interests and of simplicity of handling indicated in this chapter, and into the story form given in Chapter II? Bring a synopsis of steps to class.

4. *For junior leaders.* In view of the desire for factual detail, indicated on pages 37, 38, read the story of David's sparing of Saul's life (1 Samuel 26) and show how (in an outline of steps) you would make the story vivid pictorially, so boys and girls could imagine the scene.

CHAPTER IV

Stories for Older Groups

Between the junior age and high school age there is an intermediary stage which gives reason for the name " intermediates." In day school the boys and girls are in junior high school, a term suggesting to church-school teachers a combination of the immaturity of juniors and advancing maturity of seniors. They have not quite grown out of the junior age, yet are at times trying even harder than the seniors to be " grown up."

Their story tastes therefore range all the way from lusty adventure and slapstick comedy to the historical and idealistic. The same boys and girls who prefer the gangbuster programs on the radio are also held by biographies of men and women who have given their lives in service to humanity.

They want action. Their heroes may be Indians, Tom Sawyer, Johnny Tremain, or Florence Nightingale, but they must live adventurously. A survey of seventh-grade tastes in a large junior high school department showed stories dealing with adventure, science, history, mystery, and animals to be favorites. Such books as *Black Stallion, Bambi, My Friend Flicka, The Yearling, Lassie*, which synthesize so-called animal and human traits and relationships, appeared over and over. Growing idealism of this age reveals itself in their choices of incidents in these stories, and (among the girls) in such vocational books as *Women Will Be Doctors, Sue Barton — Neighborhood Nurse, Florence Nightingale.*

This age likes its heroes and heroines to be realistic, but they appreciate the realities of life placed in interesting — even romantic — settings.

Stories in Drama. Plays often make good stories to tell to this age (and older). All the dramatic possibilities are apparent. The climax is sure, it is easy to trace the steps leading up to it. We do not avail ourselves enough of this important source.

Stories, likewise, can make good plays and are often a springboard for creative drama in a group. We once heard Lillian Smith tell of her camp girls who, after reading *The Little Prince* imagined the Little Prince from another planet visiting a spot on ours. The problems which confronted him were new (any group could imagine them) and his two closest companions (whom the girls named " Conscience " and " Tradition ") advised him so differently that he was frequently at a loss. (In creating the dramatization the group finally decided that on this trip the Little Prince would have four companions, and their inclusion of " Science " and " Religion " was the result of discussion which led to research in the New Testament and anthropology.) One's imagination jumps ahead to possibilities in such use of stories.

We always wanted to write a story from the ideas in the Broadway play, " The Man Who Played God." He was angry at God, you remember, for not interfering to relieve a tragic situation in the lives of certain people he had observed. To get even with God, to show what God ought to be like, he takes matters into his own hands. Acting on his own just, generous, and kindly impulses, he himself interferes and changes the sad situation into a happy one.

Even the title and synopsis of this story suggest discussions on the kind of God one believes in, and the ways in which he works.

High School and Young People

Narratives which challenge thinking appeal to high school age, though of course the emotional appeal must be there. Sports stories are good, especially those which present such choices as playing the game for personal glory or for the school's tradition; striving for personal glory may lead to victory, but is it a real victory?

The stories must be plausible; magic has no place here. Facts implied must be provable. A point in favor of a popular story, " The Legend of the Black Madonna " (see Appendix) is the provable fact that the sun, shining through certain dark shades of stained glass, changes the color to gold. This story has been told in many services of worship for teen-agers and young people as well as adults.

Other services of worship which have impressed high school groups have been built around the stories of persons who have risen above physical handicaps and made life worth living — to themselves and others. These stories are culled from biographies and novels, put into story form, or used as excerpts. One, which is particularly revealing of the spiritual struggle and triumph of a cripple, is *The Little Locksmith* by Katharine Hathaway.

Realistic Situations. Both high school age and young people as a rule like to face in stories situations similar to those they might face themselves — and discuss their implications. Such a story is taken from the play " The Flaw,"[1] in which a boy and girl, driving on a lonely road, run over a tramp. The tramp is killed. Nobody saw them. Should they tell and " get into trouble " ? Should they keep still and safe — and live with their secret all their lives?

Even though the setting of a story may be unfamiliar, as in the radio Bible dramas *The Eternal Light* and *The Greatest*

---

[1] By Cyril Roberts in *Eight Prize-Winning One-Act Plays.* See Bibliography.

Story Ever Told, certain problems are recognized as universal, and recurrently to be faced. Characters in the dramas are human, like ourselves; their stories help listeners to weigh the results of one form of behavior as against another. The element of realism is strong. We can clothe greed and ambition, love and unselfishness, faith, anger and fear in clothes of any period or country. They are emotions common to mankind, duplicated on Main Street — or in the United Nations Assembly today. " Isaiah and the United Nations," [2] of *The Eternal Light* series, was a potent stab at our times from twenty-seven centuries back.

The folk tales of ancient India in the book *What Do You Think?* (see Bibliography) are outstanding for literary and narrative values, but they are included in that book for a special purpose. This purpose is the promotion of free discussion of important human problems among young people. To that end the stories were chosen and retold. Suggested questions are also given, and typical responses from members of the group before whom the stories were told. This kind of discussion is fun for teacher and pupil alike, and indicates the practical utilization of good literature as a guide in life situations.

Idealistic Stories. But we need not always be realistic. Symbolic stories in which the transfer can be easily made, as in Henry van Dyke's " The Other Wise Man," are effective as far down the age range as the twelve-to-fourteen-year-olds. High school boys and girls during the study of church history have grown in sensitivity and worshipful feeling through dramatizing stories of medieval legends such as " The Juggler of Notre Dame " (see Bibliography).

Young People and Biography.[3] Some of the best stories for

---

[2] Original radio play by Stanley H. Silverman, for the N. B. C. program, sponsored by the Jewish Theological Seminary of America. Reading version of this play is found in *The Questing Spirit*, anthology referred to at the close of this chapter.

[3] See also comments on the biographical story in chapters III and IX.

this age are of persons whose acts raise questions and provoke arguments. Muriel Lester and her gospel of peace have stirred up lively debates. An English woman who has lived through two wars, she is also a Christian.

"What is a Christian's duty in a war, anyway?" "Can't one be a Christian and help fight a war that has to be fought?"

"But fighting is killing, after all."

"Sure, you can't have a war without people getting killed, but that isn't the reason we fight."

"But you can't get around the fact that each side is out to kill the most people. Christian nations, too. And here's a woman who stands up and says, ' *It's true,* what Christ said: All men are brothers! ' So a ' Christian ' nation imprisons her."

"Well, they've got to get on with the war; what can they do but stop her influencing people?"

"Then there are times when you just have to forget you're a Christian?"

So listeners may be stirred, though they may not agree, but they are made uncomfortable — which is one of the signs that they are growing.

The story of Albert Schweitzer presents another person whose choices were important. An inspiring story of Dr. Schweitzer has been told by Joseph Gollomb in *Albert Schweitzer: Genius in the Jungle.* Musician, writer, physician — why did he choose to " bury " himself and his talents in Africa? Was it sensible? Was Jesus sensible? Is common sense the highest criterion we have?

Fictional Stories. Such dramatically written books as Sholem Asch's *The Apostle* offer splendid material for both young people and adults. Though *The Apostle* is fictional in detail, it keeps to the fact that Peter and Paul paid the supreme price for their loyalty.

And both young people and adults can be lifted to high spiritual levels by such imaginative presentations of Jesus as *Jesus the Son of Man* by Kahlil Gibran and *By an Unknown*

Disciple, published anonymously. These accounts of his contemporaries, both enemies and friends, can be expanded into longer stories, or used as springboards to discussion.

Missionary Stories.[4] Lives of missionaries have always furnished leaders with colorful and dramatic story material. The religious educator today has an obligation to present such material fairly and in the light of changes in attitude which a century and a half of missionary work have brought about.

Some of the early missionaries who went out with evangelical zeal and purpose used methods that listeners to their stories have a right to question. Their " so-sure-we-are-right " and " we-have-all-the-true-answers " attitude often offended the people of older civilizations. We have fortunately grown in world-consciousness, in perception of values in other cultures and faiths, and in consequent humility. Through the years missionaries have become students of other cultures in order to build on — not destroy — what is already there. They have learned from those they went to help, and they see their task more as the translating of one period or one culture into terms which can be universally understood.

In the name of the God of love and of healing, with the gospel of love, and with the purpose of helping people to know Jesus, instead of saving souls for Jesus, missionaries like Higginbotham, Laubach, Schweitzer, and Hubbard have gone out.

The Fan Village Project is just one illustration of missionary work organized on this principle. When Hugh Hubbard went to China he found people starving and buying prayers for rain. " Your prayers have been answered," he told the people. " I can show you how to get water," and he helped them to dig artesian wells. Religion was not mentioned until men asked him whatever made him care, and he told them " God," — as he knew him through Jesus.

[4] See also the discussion of missionary stories in Chapter IX.

Christmas Stories. " There are three strands in the Christmas tradition," J. Edgar Park reminds us in his Foreword to a little book of Christmas stories. " There is the gold thread of religion. There is the silver thread of benevolence. And then there is a gaily colored thread of homespun yarn, that's laughter." [5]

We recognize the threads in his own delightful writing, and in the many volumes of short stories printed separately or in popular collections.

For groups gathered around the Christmas tree, the storyteller looks for tales which will contribute to the happy fellowship of the occasion, telling them with zest and appreciation of their humor.

For young people's or adults' services of worship, the leader searches with a different purpose. He seeks for those which will create a " Christian " attitude towards Christmas. They may be mystical, symbolic, or realistic, but they should reflect the spirit of the one whose birthday is being celebrated; they must help the listener to distinguish in the season's abundance of gifts and opportunities the " things of most worth."

Such a story as Edna Ferber's " No Room at the Inn," which appears in *One Basket*, a collection of Miss Ferber's short stories, is an example of such present-day, realistic stories.

Two anthologies offering the richest stock of well-written stories for young people and adults are *The Fireside Book of Christmas Stories*, edited by Edward Wagenknecht and *The Questing Spirit, Religion in the Literature of Our Time*, selected by Halford E. Luccock and Frances Brentano. The first has such classics as Henry van Dyke's " The Other Wise Man," and another symbolic one of the same type, " The Man at the Gate of the World " by W. E. Cule; these are followed by a wide variety of carefully selected and highly usable stories.

[5] From *The Christmas Heretic and Other Stories.* Used by permission of The Pilgrim Press.

The Questing Spirit includes not only choice Christmas tales, but outstanding short stories and dramas culled and condensed from many sources. " Isaiah and the United Nations," referred to above, is among these. These two books are invaluable for any church-school library.

The making or adapting of stories for older groups will give the same satisfying, creative experience one has in doing it for children, if the story form and the ages of the listeners are remembered.

Suggested Assignments

1. Make a survey of reading and drama tastes of a junior, junior high or high school class, asking members to answer the questions during the week. Ask for three favorite books, three movies, three radio programs most enjoyed, and be ready to compare returns in a later class.

2. Listen yourself, critically, to religious dramas on the radio networks, to see how quickly they establish characters and situations, and awaken your curiosity about the plot.

3. Select some story which you think has possibilities for creative dramatics with your group, or find a popular stage, movie, or radio drama whose story would be a springboard for a worth-while discussion in your group.

4. Bring to class the best told missionary story you can find, or the best retelling of a New Testament story.

5. Start a file of stories to which you can turn when you need one.

CHAPTER V

Getting Ready to Tell the Story

FINDING THE RIGHT STORY

Storyteller A. You are a teacher preparing for a Sunday session. You have a textbook with a story in it for the day.

You have the aim of the " lesson "; you have studied the suggestions. You note how the story is intended to further the aim: whether it is to be used to stimulate action, start a discussion, or offer a solution to a problem already under discussion. Now you read the story.

Do you like it? Does it seem to do what it sets out to do? Is it interesting to you as a story? If it is, you will enjoy telling it, and your listeners will get all the writer put into it, plus your own appreciation. You will read it over and over to pack all the values possible into the telling.

If you do not like it, don't try to tell it — yet — for your own attitude towards it will keep the story from being effective. Analyze this attitude.

IMPROVING OR ADAPTING A STORY

1. Perhaps you have not enough background to get a " feeling " for the story. If it is based on the Bible, have you looked up all the references given and imagined yourself back in the time and place of the action? Chapters VII and VIII outline this procedure. If it is a biographical story, have you done a little research of your own?

2. Perhaps you think the story lacks " punch," or that the construction is faulty. There might be something you could do about that. Does it take too long to get into the story?

Then could you improvise a beginning which would arouse immediate interest?

3. Does it lack movement towards a climax? Then could you, knowing the point the story should make, supply the action by which a listener would be carried, step by step, to that point?

In a recent storytelling class we gave the assignment: " Study the story given in your textbook for next Sunday, and see how it could be improved."

The first teacher who reported said she thought the introduction to the story given in her book was too long. She read the story, substituting the introduction she had written. Everybody agreed that hers was far better. The textbook took six paragraphs of description before getting to the people in the story or the action. " Of course the descriptions try to provide an atmosphere," the student generously explained, " but my children would be lost after the first paragraph. So I plunged right into the story at once."

" Giving it a good start instead of a poor one," we commented, then caught sight of the cover of the textbook.

" Yes," the student admitted, " it was one of your stories."

This was (and is) an excellent time to suggest that we can often improve on the style of a given story. Adapting a story to make it more acceptable for your group is almost as satisfying an experience as creating it from scratch.

If after trials at adaptation, you find the story is still inadequate, so that you cannot put yourself whole-heartedly into its telling, you would do better to join Storyteller B or C.

Storyteller B. You are a leader in need of a certain type of story to relate to an experience, or to your study, or to a problem which has come up in the group. The right one might suggest a line of action, or stimulate a discussion, or lead to worship. You search your files until you have found one which fills your need and which you would enjoy telling — with adaptations if necessary, or without them.

For both A and B the way is now clear for preparing to tell the story.

PREPARING TO TELL THE STORY

Become Thoroughly Familiar with It. You have found the climax. Read the story again and note how each item contributes to it. Eliminate any which seem irrelevant. Read again for the beginning and ending.

Visualize your Characters. What do they look like? What are their names? What are their respective traits? Even if you are not going to describe them they must be clear in your own mind, so their actions and conversation will describe them. See them in one scene after another. One storyteller used to say she pictured in her imagination the scenes as in framed pictures on a wall. But they must have been " stills." Some would prefer visualizing motion pictures, to remind them how one bit of action leads to another or prevents another.

Make an Outline, writing out

1. Introduction: names, setting, situation, with indication of the hope or problem;

2. Action: the sequence of events which show progress towards the climax and obstacles as they are met;

3. Climax (be sure it is an answer to the curiosity and anticipation aroused in the introduction);

4. Conclusion, which winds everything up quickly and satisfyingly.

After a while you will be able to do this outlining in your mind, but even experienced storytellers often jot down these items. They aid memory and provide brief notes which can be filed to recall the story at a future time.

1. Prerequisite: Appreciation. (You've got to like your story.)

2. And you've got to <u>know</u> your story: the problem, the characters' names, appearance, characteristics.

This is the third time. I'll read it again to make sure to have the details.

3. Make an outline (on paper or in mind.) It helps you see each step in relation to the climax.

Beginning: Names, Setting, Problem, Succession of Events
First - - - - -
Second - - - - -
Third - - - - -
Climax - - - - -
Conclusion - - -

4. Practice telling story out loud. If the sound of your voice gives you stage fright, and you lose the thread, read the story again until it is yours.

5. Practice telling story to favorite child listener (in flesh or imagination), adding or omitting details appealing to age level.

6. If you are AT HOME in your story, no interruption can shake you out of your security, or your listeners' confidence in you.

INTERRUPTIONS

STORY

J.P.B.

Tell the Story to Yourself. You'll probably have forgotten some item. Go back to the book, refresh your memory, but do not concentrate on memorizing the story word for word. That would be restricting; what you are after is to impress a picture or a sequence on your mind.

Tell the story again — as often as possible — to anyone who will listen, adding conversation and details which you feel enrich the story for your particular audience.

The story is now yours. You are ready to share it appreciatively as you would an interesting or challenging experience.

CREATING YOUR OWN STORY

Storyteller C. You have searched for the right story for your Cub group, or your story hour, or your service of worship, and have not been able to find one. You must create one yourself! " How does one go about it? " you may ask.

Perhaps you have observed an incident on the playground. Perhaps a mother has told you of something that happened in her family. Perhaps a newspaper item suggests a plot. Here is one about a " rookie " patrolman who saves from drowning a boy, Leo, whose gang consider all policemen as natural enemies.

They defied the "No Skating — Danger " signs to try the frozen-over pond in the city park. Every few minutes a lookout would shout, " Scram! " when the policeman would appear and drive them off, giving them repeated warnings of the danger. Each time they returned the boys ventured farther from the edges, until the ice cracked and Leo fell in. The boys' screams for help brought the policeman, shedding cap, heavy uniform, belt and gun. The item describes how he kicked a hole in the ice at the edge, waded as far as he could and as water became too deep, swam, breaking his way through the ice crust. Leo had disappeared from the place he fell in. His head popped to the surface four or five feet farther out, disappeared, then popped up again, before the policeman grabbed him and hauled him to safety.

One Point of View. The climax will depend on whether you want it to be a hero story of a policeman, as the headlines had it;

in which event the whole story would be from his point of view. You must make your listeners so interested in the policeman that they will identify themselves with him, share his hopes, *feel* with him. He wants to make good; he can't even get the boys on his beat to respect him. He is eager for their good will: it wasn't so long since he was a boy himself, and he remembers how he felt as a boy towards policemen. He threatens, he pleads, he warns them of danger. Then he rescues one and gets a commendation. But the boys' change of attitude towards him is what makes him feel he has " arrived."

Or the story may be told from the gang's point of view. Listeners identify themselves throughout with the gang. The story begins with them, not the policeman. The climax has to do with them, not the officer. They maneuver in many ways to outwit the law and defy the police. They initiate a smaller member and instruct him in their ways and attitudes. They dare him to try the ice farther and farther out until he falls in. Then fear and guilt drive them for help and the rescue of Leo (climax) makes all policemen their friends. The change of attitude as it affects them is the end in view.

Or take the point of view of Leo himself, with the rescue giving him a new attitude about breaking laws, taking dares, or policemen in general. There are many such human interest stories in the papers which supply enough details to make the creation of your story easy.

The first thing to do is to determine what point you want to bring out, and through what character you wish to bring it out. Then start your story with that character and tell it from his viewpoint. For instance, if you chose the policeman's point of view, you would keep to his movements, his motives, his reactions. You would not tell what Leo or the gang thought and felt, except as their reactions were observed by the policeman.

In the same way, in telling the story from the gang's point of view, all you would know about the policeman's would be through the gang's idea of it; for example, " There he was with his old stick. Who did he think he was, anyway? " *Not* " They urged Leo nearer the ice. A policeman on the beat came around the corner. ' Hello,' thought the policeman, ' there are those boys again. How can I? . . .' " etc.

A fourth viewpoint might be that of a narrator, who would see everything objectively, reporting only what actually happened or was said. You would not describe thoughts or feelings of any of the characters, because you would be only an observer of what went on. The listeners, too, become observers.

Further illustration of writing from one point of view or another will be found in Chapter VIII, STORIES OF JESUS.

Here are other headlines which lure one to read details for story material:

a) BOY DREAMS HERO'S ROLE — WAKES TO FIND IT TRUE
SAVES OCCUPANTS OF HOTEL FROM FIRE

b) FRESH AIR FUND ALUMNUS PAYS BACK A " DEBT "
Now an Executive, He Helps Raise Money for Others at Model Train
Exhibit.

c) BOY, 11, FINDS $20.00 AND PROVES HIS HONESTY
He Turns It in to Police Despite Family's Poverty and a Forlorn Christmas.

What stories these suggest! Let us use the last one to " build " a story step by step.

Determining a Climax. Unlike the policeman story, the climax is already determined for us. " He turns the money in to the police." We must fill in the steps leading up to that point. We need to decide what would make him turn it in (causation), and what would make it hard for him to do so. The climax must be plausible but not obvious. The possibility of the final decision must be inherent in the early part of the story, but the reason for another decision must be evident too. This provides for uncertainty and struggle.

We know that he was poor; that money would be needed for food and rent, and that Christmas was near. Yet he turned it in. Why? We try out possible influences.

Was it conscience? His mother's or the church's teaching about honesty? The example of a hero? Acquaintance with the law about finding lost property? That last seems most likely, without knowing more of the boy's background. He knew about the police. Then let's build on that. We're ready to start on an outline.

Introduction. (This answers the three necessary questions, Who? When? Where? We get him placed.) We name him — Joe. He shines shoes to help buy food for his mother and little sister. It is near Christmas in a big city. As he leaves home that morning he says cheerily as usual that maybe he'll make a lot of money that day. (Pleasing, hopeful nature established. Listeners will reflect Joe's anticipation and hope with him.)

Sequence of Events. 1. Goes downstairs, whistling, into the street.

2. Passes Police Station. (We introduce causation element early, so events which follow will seem natural.) Salutes Sergeant Sullivan just coming out. Police are his friends. Always salutes them. Sometimes he goes inside to chat with them. He watches them as people come in to get help; hears them answering telephone calls about lost dogs, lost children, lost money. They tell him they're Guardians of the Law, and today Sergeant Sullivan walks along with him, asks how he's coming on. Joe tells him he wants to make a lot of money today, to get his mother a big dinner and sister a doll for Christmas. Leaves Sergeant. Pauses to look in Christmas window, sets up shoe-shine box, starts business. End of day, counts money. Enough for a part of the rent, and a little more. " Oh, well, perhaps tomorrow will be better."

3. Starts home. Finds flattened wallet on trolley track. $20.00 inside. Visions of Christmas fun, food, rent, movies, etc. (Accentuate this, to make decision more difficult.) Wonders who dropped wallet — realizes it belonged, still belongs, to someone. It isn't his! But nobody saw him pick it up. . . . Pauses at red light, salutes policeman, " Guardian of the Law." There's a law about turning in lost property.

4. Walks slowly, then faster. Passes Christmas window without looking towards it. Police Station. Sergeant Sullivan there. Greets him with question about money he expected to make today. (Another moment of hesitation.)

Climax. Joe turns in wallet, but doesn't linger. Must buy groceries for supper. Goes out light-hearted at something Sergeant Sullivan said.

Conclusion. As he bursts into his tenement home, calls cheerfully, " Hi, Mom! Here's food and part of the rent. Say, I found some money and turned it in to the police. What do you think they said . . . that I'd make a good policeman myself someday! "

There could be other conclusions. Knowing the generosity of police, it would be quite natural for Sergeant Sullivan, acquainted with the needs of Joe's family, to see that he got one of the Christmas baskets the station provided for the needy in the neighborhood. This would not come as a reward for honesty, but would just happen. And it would provide the smaller listeners with a very happy ending when they thought all was lost.

Storyteller C would prepare this story for telling just as A and B would theirs. After writing it out he would go over and over the sequences, visualizing characters and action, finding a good beginning and ending, and practicing the " tricks of the storyteller's trade " described in the next chapter.

SUGGESTED ASSIGNMENTS

1. Make an outline, according to steps, of the story your course of study suggests for next Sunday's session. Decide how you would begin the story if you were writing the story for your own group.

2. Find a story in or outside your textbook, which would supplement and add meaning to an experience the group is having. Make an outline of the steps and indicate what changes you would make, if any, in telling it.

3. Expand an incident observed or reported, or one of the headlines on page 58, into a story outline. Determine the climax and write a beginning which would point towards it.

The class has now become a workshop. The more the students practice and criticize their own and each other's efforts, the more valuable the class sessions become. Suggested Assignments from now on will assume that the larger part of each session is given over to students' participation.

CHAPTER VI

Telling the Story

TELLING *versus* READING

As a storyteller you have the advantage over the one who reads a story. There is nothing between you and your listeners. You look directly into their faces. There is a rapport established between you not possible when you are following the printed page. You are not bound by the phrasing of the author, but are telling his story in your own words. You are communicating something worth while. Your coming upon it was a delightful (enlightening, worshipful) experience for you; you want to share it. That others may share it fully, you study the ways of making your story effective.

Comfort. You take care that your listeners are comfortable. They can all see your face, so continual scraping of chairs or craning of necks will not be necessary. They can all hear your voice, for you speak to the back row, not the front. The ventilation must be good, or at the end of what you consider a successful effort, you may look at faces flushed with heat rather than interest, and the only comment you will hear will be like Freddie's " I'm thweat'n'."

You are comfortable yourself. Your collar is not too tight, your belt needs no adjustment. You know your story; every character is clear to you, every scene is a picture in your mind, every act is a part of a sequence leading to a climax. Your own mastery of the situation arouses confidence in your listeners that you know where you are going.

Naturalness. If standing, do not strike an unusual attitude, but stand in a natural position (natural for good posture, of course, with feet together and hands at ease). If sitting, your manner is intimate and conversational. If it is natural for you to use gestures with hands or body, use them, but do not force or overdo them for what you think is dramatic effect. You are telling a story, not acting. Anything which comes between the story and the listener is bad. Your desire to make your story dramatic might mean that you are spotlighting your own ego, instead of the story.

Do not use meaningless gestures. Leave beads and buttons alone; keep hands quiet, or they, too, may divert attention. You remember the story of the judge whose idle tearing of paper into bits throughout the defense testimony so distracted the jury that they hardly heard it and brought in a verdict that won the case for the prosecuting attorney.

Voice. Speak in a natural tone of voice, but project it. Do not keep it caged in the roof of your mouth or back in your throat. Breathe deeply, from the diaphragm, and your voice will project itself more surely.

Avoid honeyed accents. Cultivate variety of tone; children loathe monotony. " How would you like it," a junior girl once asked a leader, " if your teacher just went ' ooooooooooo ' all the time? I like people to go ' oo oo oo oo oo oo .' "

In telling stories to children, imitate sounds indicated in your story, winds blowing, thunder rumbling, dogs barking. Part of the attraction of *The Little Engine That Could* lies in the variety of sounds the engines make. Change your voice to suit the age and character of the one speaking. One can hardly imagine the Three Bears all using the same voice as they go through their house after Goldilocks has been there.

Hurry when swift action is indicated. Let your voice reflect wonder, strength, joy, as called for. Use pauses for impressiveness or to increase suspense.

Never let your voice get flat; you will see interest waver. Remember you are communicating something, not reciting.

Look at Audience. Speak directly to the audience as in a conversation, looking at them instead of over their heads into space. Avoid, however, fixing your glance on one victim until he squirms. Take in the whole audience as you talk, so there will be no danger of a child on the outskirts begging, at the close, " Now tell it to *me!* "

Tell the Story Creatively. Use your imagination in the telling, and your listeners will use theirs. Someone has said, "A story is not what you say, but what you see; it is not what a child hears, but what he sees."

Though storytelling is not acting, the unfolding of a story is like the unfolding of a drama. But a play has scenery and characters and off-stage devices to help create realism. The storyteller must, single-handed, supply sights and sounds and actions of the drama. She must make each character come alive, every scene clear and vivid. If you are a beginner, keep your outline in your hand so you will not wander off the path of sequence.

MAKE THE CHARACTERS COME ALIVE

They will not come to life merely by your talking about them; for example: " Jesus was always helping people "; " David was a brave boy "; " The disciples learned a great many lessons about helping people." The storyteller may *say* that a person is thus and so, but that does not convince us. We want to see the person in action, we need to hear him speak; then we can judge for ourselves. We must in our imagination *see* Jesus in the act of causing a sick man to rise from his bed and walk. Let us *see* David killing that lion that threatened his flock. We want to be in the room where Jesus got water and a towel, and *see* him act out a lesson.

Keep Your Characters Moving. Let them describe themselves. Note, in the following excerpt, how much is told about these characters entirely by what they do and say.

Now it so happened one day that a man came to Chihua who was rich and big and drove a motor car, and he knew beautiful things when he saw them.

"Aaaah, ooooh," sang the singing potter, rolling his pushcart down the road, "Aaaah, ooooh."

"How much?" called a woman, stopping the cart and shifting her baby on her hip.

"Five cents. A bowl to keep rice and beans for a whole family. . . ."

"¡Hé!" cried the woman, "five cents is a great sum for a bowl."

"But not for a singing potter's bowl. Happiness —"

"Say four cents."

"Happiness goes with it. Joy —"

"Wait," cried the big rich man, getting out of his car. "Wait; I'll give you fifty cents for that bowl."

Now in all the history of Chihua no one had ever said such a thing as this. But the potter stood firm.

"Five cents," he said, looking at the woman.

"Here," she replied, slipping the coin into the potter's hand.

"A dollar," shouted the big rich man.

"Ah, señor, it is sold." [1]

The author has depended for her effect much more on verbs than on adjectives, and on the speech of the characters themselves, rather than any observations about them.

[1] From "The Singing Potter," by Dorothy F. McConnell in *Sugar Is Sweet* by M. E. Forsyth and D. F. McConnell. Quoted in *Missionary Stories to Tell*, The Friendship Press. Used by permission.

USE DIRECT DISCOURSE

Nothing makes a character come alive more than the use of direct discourse: "And he said unto them " — Jesus' voice is almost heard in what follows. The stories would sound quite different if the narrator had used indirect discourse: " He told them that —", " He reminded them that —", or " He asked him what the law said and the lawyer told him that it said to love God with all one's heart and all one's soul and all one's strength and all one's mind, and one's neighbor as oneself. Jesus told him he had answered correctly and if he did that he would live."

Supposing the author of " The Singing Potter " had written:

The rich man got out of his car and went towards the potter. He could not persuade him to sell the bowls. He told him he would be famous and rich, but when the potter still refused, he went back to his car, thinking the potter was stupid, while the potter thought him just as stupid.

That was not the way Dorothy McConnell told the story. She makes us see pictures, and hear speech, and feel personalities.

"Come, come! " cried the big rich man impatiently. " I will buy all your pottery, . . . and I will pay you much, much money to make bowls and jugs and pots like these."

"But then," objected the potter, " what would the people of Chihua do for their pots and bowls and jugs? ". . . .

"You would become famous if you worked for me. And certainly you would be rich."

"Señor," and the potter shook his head and looked troubled, " I know nothing about all that. It sounds very strange to me. I make my wares for Chihua." And he shrugged his shoulders politely. . . .

" Oh, these stupid natives," said the big rich man to himself as he drove his car down the road. " They will not do what is for their own good."

"Ah, these stupid foreigners," said the singing potter to himself as he trundled his cart up the hill. " They think that money is everything." . . .

HOW TO TORTURE YOUR LISTENERS

HOW TO TORTURE YOUR LISTENERS

"Aaah, oooh," came the sound of the singing potter's voice from the road beyond Chihua. "Honk! Honk! " went the big rich man's motor horn.[2]

Direct discourse here is even carried to the motor horn, to make the final picture vivid, leaving the listener to make his own appraisal of the characters and their viewpoints.

USE " ACTION " VERBS

In conversations in your story, choose verbs that in themselves describe a character's appearance or mood. It is the movement in the verb that makes the character come to life, and incidentally avoids wordiness.

" Well," he grumbled, " I'll do it this once."

We see him. He is living, breathing, scowling. You know how he feels. That one verb " grumbled " tells as much as if a paragraph were used to describe him.

Compare the following two ways of showing a reaction. Which is more alive? Which makes you feel more awe?

1. " Not *really?* " she gasped.

2. Marcia couldn't believe it.

So also, " she sighed," " he bellowed," " she wavered," " she panted," picture living, breathing persons. Verbs are alive. Her eyes *blazed*. His fists *tightened*. Her dimples *twinkled*. His steps *lagged*. Her gaze *wandered*.

MAKING SCENES VIVID

In drama there are lights, color, and properties to create the proper atmosphere and give realism. The story must supply this atmosphere. It is like a game, trying to find words which will immediately conjure up settings and give the desired im-

[2] From " The Singing Potter."

pression. Study Anne Lindbergh's *North to the Orient* to see what words can do to make you see and feel; or the Cratchits' Christmas dinner in Dickens' *Christmas Carol*, to make you smell and taste! This is fun. Put your creative imagination to work — or play.

There is a point in your story where it is quiet. How quiet? Make your listeners almost stop breathing for fear they will disturb it. " It was so still you could have heard the new grass growing."

It is a hot day. How will your audience know? Can you make them realize it through every sense until they *hear* it with the midsummer insects buzzing at their ears, and *feel* it in the torrid breeze, and *taste* it in the dry dust, and *smell* it in the heavy scents from the garden, and *see* it in the dripping brows, until the audiences' tongues are hanging out, and they're reaching for fans?

That sense appeal is important. To make an impression clear ask yourself, What would it look like, feel like, sound like? Did it have a taste, an odor? What were they like?

In Frances Weld Danielson's book, *The Practice Storytelling Class*, the teacher says, " Describe a giant so I shall see him."

Ready-to-Try: Once there was a big, tall man.

Leader: I don't see him.

Ready-to-Try: He was very tall.

Leader: I don't care.

Quick-as-a-Flash: Don't you care if he was as tall as the moon?

Leader: Yes, I do. Now you've done it. You've given me something with which to measure my giant. Can somebody do this without exaggeration?

Ready-to-Try: A giant is at least a foot taller than a tall man.

Leader: You forget that I'm posing as a small child, and that to me a foot means only the foot on the end of a leg.

Sluggard: A giant is taller than the tallest man you ever saw. Once a giant stood beside a man and he put his elbow on the man's head.

Quick-as-a-Flash: Once there was a giant, and he was as tall as this (*raising her hand high above her head*).

Cynic: There was a giant who was so tall that when he lay down he had to put his feet out of the window.

Leader: Splendid! Do you know what you three have done? You've used comparison and gesture and action, to make me see your giant. All of them are good storytelling methods.[3]

CREATING SUSPENSE

We know how important the suspense element is in story, motion picture, or drama. Remember the story lacks " punch " without it. A boy wants something. As you tell the story, make him want it terribly. Make your listeners feel with him that life just won't be worth living if he can't have it. He has thought of it, dreamed of it, saved for it for weeks. Don't let him get it too easily! Put plausible obstacles in his path, even if they are imaginary obstacles which occur to you, one after another. They will be real to him, likewise to your listeners. Make the realization of his dream a tremendous relief because of the uncertainties you have emphasized.

If you are telling a biographical story you will be working towards a climax, whether the story is to be told as a whole or serially. If serially, each chapter, though a step towards the grand climax, should have its own high point, which is reached through difficulty. Make the difficulty the point of struggle towards accomplishment of that one step.[4]

Gentle Student, if the story you have chosen — from fiction, biography, or text — lacks the dramatic element to make it " come alive," bring it to life yourself by your own creative imagination, supplying it with vitamins of direct discourse,

[3] From *The Practice Storytelling Class,* Frances W. Danielson. The Pilgrim Press. Used by permission.
[4] See also Chapter III, page 41; Chapter IX, page 101.

action verbs, vivid picturing, comparisons and contrasts — and suspense. Note how the story, " The Still, Small Voice " (see Appendix), is told imaginatively, using rhythm and contrast effectively in building up to its high point — the answer to Elijah's problem.

QUESTIONS AND INTERRUPTIONS

The children's storyteller who asks a rhetorical question in the midst of her story must expect anything but a rhetorical answer. We think the lady in California who interrupted the story of the Flood to ask of a child more engrossed in showing off her new dress, "Anna-Marie, what would you say if it rained forty days and forty nights without stopping? " deserved the response, " I'd say it was very unusual."

But when the questions come from the children, they are often contributions and indicate interest and attention. Children's comments are usually not interruptions. Sometimes they show how much they are identifying themselves with the story — of a boy named John, for instance: " My brother's name is John "; or of Chinese children playing jackstones: " I play that game."

Sometimes their questions are for clarification. " What does that word mean? " " Miss ———, you use such big words my head goes round and round." Welcome such " interruptions " and learn from them not to soar above their spinning heads.

TWO DON'T'S

In telling your story, if you suddenly discover you've left out an important point, DON'T try to correct yourself with, " Oh, I forgot to say. . . ." You confuse and may lose your audience. Bring in the item as naturally as you can wherever it best fits into the sequence, as if you'd meant it to be there all along.

And DON'T tack on a moral to your tale!

Assignments for Story Workshop

1. Let a member of the class volunteer to tell a story badly. (**Don't all** speak at once.) Find ten things wrong with this performance.

2. Reconstruct the poorly told story to make it an **artistic** whole.

3. Listen to a well-told story and count its good points.

4. Make the class hear, from your use of words, a sound that is frightening.

5. Describe the approach of a child, a motor truck, a circus parade, so your audience can hear and see each.

6. Make the class feel a) hungry
   b) suffocating with heat
   c) the relief after a cool shower.

7. A Multiple Choice Test. Imagine yourself as a storyteller to a group of primary children. You are approaching the climax of your story, saying, " The King had an iron will. He spoke sternly to the soldier," when one child pipes up, " What's an iron will? " and another, " What does *sternly* mean? " Which would you do:

> Stop and explain?
> Send the children out for interrupting?
> Pretend you didn't hear and go on with the story?
> Go home and revise your vocabulary?

8. An Assignment to End All Assignments:

> When the rules are mastered, *practice!* The best way to learn how to tell stories is *to tell stories*.

CHAPTER VII

Bible Stories

Compilers, illustrators, script writers, and professional story-tellers have long been aware of the attraction that Bible stories have for the public. Commercial artists and publishing houses realize their sales value, the motion picture and radio see their dramatic possibilities. Storytellers, always seeking to introduce children to good literature and great heroes, find both in the Bible. Their programs include its stories as they do other epic tales from many cultures.

Their Place in Religious Education

To the teacher in religious education the Bible is also a source book for dramatic tales, but it is more. Our purpose in using it is different from that of other storytellers, and therefore our basis for the selection of material is different.

To the religious educator, the Bible is the story of a people's recognition of a mysterious, controlling, loving Power in the universe, and their efforts to understand this Power and relate themselves to it. It is the one source for the story and teachings of Jesus reported by those who were closest to him during his public ministry, and who themselves felt the direct impact of his life and personality.

Because the wonderings, struggles, and seekings of a people have a universal quality, there are times in our lives when our experiences match theirs in spirit, and it is profitable to know where they looked, progressively, for answers to their questions about life; how they felt when they faced the great

73

mysteries, how they learned to meet the problems of living together.

Teachers working closely with children know at what stage in their development or their study a story from the Bible will supplement a group experience, by suggesting an answer to a problem or a way of acting, or by bringing about a new appreciation. This would not ordinarily be below primary age. Storytelling in the nursery and kindergarten demands so much simplification and is so individual that the teacher finds that stories closer to a little child's life can be more effective.

In *The Use of the Bible with Children,* chapters V-VIII, Ethel Smither reminds us of children's limitations as well as their abilities at different age levels. We should be aware of the harm that may be done in introducing Bible stories too early, and how, if we oversimplify them to meet the child's level, we are doing violence to the stories themselves.

Bible stories we tell should be selected for their appropriateness to our situation and their ability to add to growing understandings and appreciations.

THEIR PURPOSE IN LESSON MATERIALS

Stories in our textbooks usually have specific purposes. They are designed to parallel some part of the learning experience (which the textbook writer has also suggested), to start discussions concerning these, or to indicate answers to problems likely to be raised.

The teacher with her course book in her hand, preparing for the coming session, reads the purpose for which the writer included the story. The only reason for its inclusion was to further that purpose, and this is also the teacher's only reason for telling it.

Classes are unpredictable. No course writer can meet the story requirements for every class at all times. If, at this point, the class purpose is different from that of the writer of the course of study, another story or no story would be better than an unsuitable one. A teacher will not twist a story's meaning to suit her ends. She will instead try to find one which will meet the class's needs.

FINDING A SUITABLE STORY

A third-grade teacher found herself and her class at a standstill in the course of a project which had been undertaken enthusiastically enough. One by one the children had lost interest, discouraged by failures or wearied by the work entailed.

It *was* a difficult undertaking, the teacher admitted to herself, as she was considering plans for the next Sunday. But it was not impossible, if each child did the work he had volunteered to do, if they all worked together, " each helping his neighbor." That was the way Nehemiah had built the walls of Jerusalem!

This was the story that immediately came to her mind to meet the problem of group co-operation: a perennial problem, as she, a well-seasoned teacher, knew. Where was the story retold in the course text? She knew she had seen it. Unfortunately, the planners of her text had not foreseen that at this particular time this particular class would need Nehemiah's strategy. " Co-operation " and Nehemiah were treated in another quarter. The files were at the church. The teacher was at home. " Oh, well . . ." Sooner or later the good teacher who plans a Bible story for her class goes to the source, to steep herself in as much background as possible. If the " story for the day " had been of Nehemiah, her procedure would have been the same. She took up her Bible and reread the first six chapters of Nehemiah, visualizing the dramatic scenes and action.

Here in this story was a task to be done which seemed insurmountable, yet which, because of good organization and the willingness of everyone to work on his special assignment, was accomplished in unbelievable time. But it was not completed without discouragements and weariness and fears — enemies were at work outside and inside — and not without need of rallying calls, reminders of the importance of their work. These were what made the story applicable to the class!

The teacher reviewed it all. Details were prolific, the climax was clear. The wall was built in fifty-two days! She must first make her listeners realize the size of the task and the reason for it, so they would feel the initial hopelessness of it, then want to roll up their sleeves and go at it themselves.

Should she tell the story in parts, the first part one day, climaxing that with the permission, blessing, and soldiers of Artaxerxes? She read the story in both the American Standard and the Moffatt versions, delighting in the latter's use of quotation marks which pointed up the direct discourse.

Or should she tell it in one session, beginning with the request of the king's cup-bearer? The children might remember Nehemiah in connection with the reading of the Law and the Thanksgiving Proclamation. This recollection would be the preparation for the story.

She turned again to the account of that preliminary survey of Nehemiah's. It took three days and a night. There were miles of rubble, huge stones toppling over each other, charred remains of arched gates, bolts and hinges twisted by fire, cluttered heaps which left no place for his beast to step. One of the great blocks of stone in his path would take the strength and skill of many to lift. How could the thousands of blocks ever be assembled again into the high thick wall which it once had been?

The teacher rode with Nehemiah that night. She, herself, became oppressed with the magnitude of his task. So must Nehemiah have been, and the remnant of Jews in Jerusalem, until they caught his enthusiasm and purpose at his rallying call. " You see the plight we are in — Jerusalem lying in waste and the gates burned with fire. Come, let us rebuild the wall! " So they set their hands bravely to the good work. (The " pep talk," as one of the boys called it, made the people undertake their task in the same spirit of enthusiasm that had launched the class on its project.)

But there were discouragements and temptations to abandon the job. Even with the division of labor, each family having its share (the teacher would go into detail here about the portion undertaken by each, with even the women working), it must have seemed a hopeless task at times. The teacher would stress the annoyances and burdensomeness, and bring in the voices of those who scoffed and accused and threatened.

There were plots, of which Nehemiah was warned (this would be a dramatic bit). " Let us meet . . . in the temple," he was urged; " they are coming to kill you — yes, coming to kill you by night! " Nehemiah's answer would show the caliber of man he was without her ever describing him: " Is a man like me to run away? Besides, who would go into the temple, simply to save his life? I will not go in! " [1]

Probably the worst of the obstacles was that the work was hard (as were parts of the class project). The people must have grown tired. And they had other things they wanted to do (like the class). They had to be rallied again to the cause, when the wall was halfway up; reminded of their original purpose, re-inspirited. Neither Nehemiah nor the workers deserted. They built the wall in less than two months!

Thus a teacher finds a Bible story which will fit into a class situation. And having found it, she can work it up into good story form before preparing to tell it.

Bible Stories and Worship

Leaders of worship have their own purposes, and the more closely related they are to the work of the classes participating, the more helpful the stories will be in connecting worship with

[1] Neh. 6: 10-11. From *The Bible: A New Translation* by James Moffatt. Copyright 1935 by Harper & Brothers. Used by permission.

class experiences. Whatever the leader's aim, and whatever the story, to carry the message, it must be suited to the age-group listening.

ASSOCIATION WITH PERSONALITIES

Bible passages can be filled with association through stories of their use by others. The nineteenth psalm will always be associated with Michael Pupin, after one has read his story *From Immigrant to Inventor* and learned how this psalm which his mother taught him grew in meaning through his life.

The verses: " The earth is the Lord's, and the fulness thereof " and " I will lift up mine eyes unto the hills," had special significance to George Washington Carver and his story brings this out. (See Rackham Holt's *George Washington Carver* and Shirley Graham and George Lipscomb's *Doctor George Washington Carver: Scientist.*) Both junior and older primary children have been enriched by these stories.

STORIES AS BACKGROUNDS FOR THE PSALMS

An original story of the making of a psalm or litany may lead to more worshipful use of a psalm itself, or to the creating of one by the children. It is not difficult for the leader to imagine how such a psalm as Psalm 136 was created, or a cumulative one like Psalm 150. As ballads and spirituals have grown through the contribution of one person or group after another, with many joining in a common refrain, so many of these psalms or litanies probably grew. The imagined story may revolve around one in a band of people who makes the final contribution as a climax. Again, the storyteller may assume a psalm to be the outgrowth of one person's or one group's fresh reason for praise.

It is misleading to ascribe all the so-called Psalms of David to David himself. A poet and musician, such a claim was a tribute to his gifts, but internal evidence puts many psalms in other periods. One teacher introduces a story of the twenty-third psalm:

Hundreds of years ago there lived in Palestine a shepherd boy who later became a king. His name was David and the stories say that he was a great singer and that he could make music on the harp. He made so many songs that years afterwards, when people collected all the beautiful songs they and their fathers and grandfathers had sung, they called them all the Songs of David. Nobody knows which songs he really wrote, but they must have been very beautiful to make people say, long after, when they heard a particularly lovely one, " David must have written that." Because King David had once been a shepherd boy, this is the way I like to think that one of the most beautiful songs happened to be sung.

Harriet W. Marr has imagined a whole series of such possible origins for certain psalms, just as she has imagined situations which were helped by the use of other psalms. (See " Be Still . . . and Know That I Am God," in the Appendix.)

PSALM TWENTY-FOUR AS A BASIS FOR A STORY

One does not need to depend on the imagination entirely, however, for origins of some of the psalms. One of the most dramatic, for which a junior teacher can look up the probable background in her own Bible, is the twenty-fourth. It invites antiphonal participation and the juniors enjoy dramatizing it. The title affixed to it in the American Standard Version is " The King of Glory Entering Zion," and it was probably occasioned by David's bringing the Ark of the Covenant to Jerusalem. The ark had special significance to the descendants of the tribes which Moses led through the wilderness, for it was a symbol of God's presence among them. The teacher must get the feeling of this significance before she tells her story. Let us follow her progress as she puts this into story form.

For Background. The teacher looks up "Ark " in her Bible concordance, finds " Sacred Ark " and follows up the references as to its origin, its building, its use as a shrine, its loss, its restoration, its twenty years in the " house of Abinadab in the hill," its three months in the house of Obed-edom, its transfer to Jerusalem to the tent prepared for it by David, and its final resting place in Solomon's temple. (This is a story of the period when the Jewish people believed God abode in a certain place, to be noted by the teacher.)

For Detail. If a commentary is available the teacher looks up the comments on Psalm 24. There will be a reference to another account of David's bringing the ark to Jerusalem. She reads and is thrilled by the colorful details of 1 Chronicles 13: 1-14; 15; 16: 1. She can see that procession and hear the cymbals and the singing. The rest of the background has helped her to feel the importance of the event. There is abundance of material here to make a story. The teacher's task is that of selection.

Choosing the Climax. Since the reason for the procession which used this psalm is the desire of David and the people to have the ark in Jerusalem, the fulfillment of that desire will be the climax, 1 Chronicles 16: 1. "And they brought in the ark of God and set it in the midst of the tent. . . ."

Introduction. Here we find David, now king, thinking of this symbol of God's presence which had meant in earlier years so much to his people (a brief description of the ark would prevent the children from confusing it with Noah's ark), and greatly feeling the need of it, "for we sought not unto it in the days of Saul." They had missed it, and the people had gone astray.

Body of Story. The steps might be as follows:

1. David's proposal to war council, assembling "all Israel to bring the ark";

2. Removal of ark from Abinadab on the new cart, music and dancing accompanying procession;

3. Incident at Chidon. Why David left the ark at home of Obed-edom (obstacle 1, detail depending on group and their ability to interpret the superstition);

4. David's preparing a site for ark in Jerusalem, pitching tent for it;

5. Gathering of Israel, distributing duties, purification of priests and Levites; choristers appointed;

6. Procession at gates — forgetting password (obstacle 2);

7. Remembering, gates opening (climax).

Conclusion. So they brought in the ark . . . and put it in its place, inside the tent that David had pitched for it.

Elizabeth Colson in her *Second Primary Book in Religion* captured the splendor and excitement of the procession and the psalm in a story prepared for children even younger than juniors. We quote from her version to show how the story form has been followed, and how she suited vocabulary and details to the age she was writing for. The children following her course would have heard the story of the wilderness wandering, of Moses going up the mountain to talk with God, and getting directions for erecting the tent tabernacle and making the ark; and God's promise, "There I will meet with thee."

She begins with David's remembering the story forgotten by a new generation. She omits the scene at Chidon, but includes details which show she had studied the references and a commentary until she could *feel* the story.

. . . As David wondered what he could do to help his people . . . he remembered the story of the tent church in the wilderness. He had loved that story when he was a boy, and now as he thought about it, he remembered the ark, and that God had said to Moses, "There I will meet with thee."

David knew that was just what the people of Jerusalem needed — to be reminded to be good, brave, and true, as we are by the American flag when we see it waving above us. He knew that when they saw the gold box they would know that God was with them. So David made a plan to bring the ark to Jerusalem. There was no beautiful temple for it to be kept in, but David had a tent of fine cloth made, and put up on the hill of Jehovah near his palace, for the ark. He remembered that the children of Israel had called God "The King of glory," and he said, "They need a king more wonderful than I am; they need a King of glory."

For years and years the ark had been left in a house way down in the country and the people in that house had been very happy, for God had been with them.

One morning a splendid procession went out through the city gates, to walk down into the country and bring the ark back to Jerusalem. David was clothed in a robe of fine linen and the priests were in the robes they wore when they preached to the people. They carried a fine soft blue cloth to cover the ark, for they wanted to keep it free from dust as they walked back to Jerusalem over the dry roads and the hot fields. A company of soldiers went too, and as they passed out through the gates the soldiers on the wall gave them the password.

Down through the lovely country they went, and they found the house where the ark was. Four priests lifted it and the others covered it carefully with the blue cloth. Then up through the country they walked, and it was springtime. The trees were covered with new buds, and the grass was soft and new, and the priests and soldiers saw these things and were glad. They knew now that God was with them, for the ark reminded them that God had said, " There I will meet with thee."

They were so happy and excited that one of the soldiers called out, " The earth is the Lord's, and the fulness thereof! " and somebody answered, " The world, and they that dwell therein! " Others shouted,

> " For he hath founded it upon the seas,
> And established it upon the floods! "

When the procession came near Jerusalem they could see that a great many people had come out of the city to meet them. The men and women and children came running and shouting for joy. They had brought their harps and their cymbals and their trumpets and there was music and gladness. Suddenly one of the people called out: " Who shall ascend into the hill of the Lord? And who shall stand in his holy place? " And the others answered, " He that hath clean hands, and a pure heart! "

The procession came up to the city gates and halted. The gates were closed. The people were impatient. They wished to march up through the streets of Jerusalem and see the ark placed in the tent that David had made ready for it. The soldiers on the wall did not move, and the people called out,

> " Lift up your heads, O ye gates;
> And be ye lifted up, ye everlasting doors,
> And the King of glory will come in! "

The soldiers wanted the password, so they called down, " Who is the King of glory? "

" The Lord strong and mighty, the Lord mighty in battle! " cried the people. But that was not the word, so the gates did not open. Then the people called again, " Lift up your heads, O ye gates; yea, lift them up, ye everlasting doors: And the King of glory will come in." Again the soldiers on the walls asked, " Who is this King of glory? " The soldiers in the procession tried to remember what the soldiers on the wall had said as they marched away that morning, but the day had been so full of interesting things that they could not remember. They looked about at the crowds of people and saw that there were hosts and hosts of them.

They remembered the hosts and hosts of people in the world and that the Lord was with them all and that they were his people and the sheep of his pasture. Then one of them remembered and cried aloud, "The Lord of hosts!" and the others joined him and said, "The Lord of hosts! He is the King of glory!" That was the password! That was what the soldiers had been told to say! The gates began to rise. Slowly they were lifted up, and the people crowded into the city streets. They followed the procession up and up through the streets of Jerusalem until they came to the Hill of the Lord, and with shoutings and the sound of trumpets they set the ark in the tent which David had made for it.[2]

IMAGINATION IN BIBLE STORIES

Not all stories in the Bible are as full of detail to help a teacher in the retelling as that of Nehemiah, or the bringing of the ark to Jerusalem. In fact, many a so-called Bible story has no more foundation than one short verse of Scripture.

There are certain standards we are bound to observe in using biblical material imaginatively. The most important is that our story must be *true to the spirit of the text*.

We remember a lesson story which was written "to teach obedience to parents." The title was "Joseph, a Boy Who Did an Errand for His Father," and the author overworked her imagination on the details of the boy's cheerful obedience to his father's command to go hunting for his brothers. The implication was, of course, that all listeners would feel impelled to rush home from Sunday school to obey their parents cheerfully. Aside from its utter ineffectiveness to motivate any such conduct, it did rank violence to the story itself. It would have been truer to the spirit of the story if the author had used her imagination on details which would show what made Joseph's brothers want to get rid of him and his boasts.

Many Old Testament stories are epic in their quality. A teacher is not justified in taking a single incident out of its context and misrepresenting characters and story to suit her purpose. At that period of Joseph's career he needed discipline,

---

[2] From *A Second Primary Book in Religion* by Elizabeth Colson. Abingdon-Cokesbury Press. Used by permission of Anne M. Colson.

not emulation. Life gave him the discipline, and it is his life story that is significant. The errand was important as an incident in the development of the story and of Joseph, but not as an example of obedience to parents.

The Old Testament stories related their characters' deeds quite objectively. Some would reflect to the hero's credit, judged by what we call Christian standards, some to his shame by any standard. Therein lies the universality of the stories' appeal. Therein, too, lies their value to teachers of religion. Each one of us is a combination of weaknesses and strength, failing often to live up to the best we know, needing forgiveness frequently, yet capable of greatness because of our relation to God. Each of us needs to grow at some point. Ideas and attitudes of many adults show an immaturity to match children's, and the level of children's thinking, in their beliefs or fears, corresponds with that of some of the people in the Old Testament stories.

The Bible covers over a thousand years of growing concepts of God, men's relationship to him and to their fellow men. Its stories have their greatest value when seen in the light of ever-enlarging concepts and deepening insights.

ASSIGNMENTS FOR STORY WORKSHOP

1. Come prepared to listen to stories told by members of the group. Make a list of strong points for which to look in the storyteller's rendering, and be ready to suggest how weak points could be strengthened.

2. Come prepared to tell the story you expect to use next Sunday, or at your next meeting of the group you lead.

3. If you are not at present in charge of any group, come prepared to tell before the class any story which you think has religious value.

4. *For all in the class.* Bring a Bible or New Testament to the next session. If you have other versions besides the American Standard, bring these, as there are sure to be plenty of this and the King James version. Be sure that somebody brings a concordance, and that another brings a harmony of the gospels; another a commentary or Bible dictionary. (See titles listed in Bibliography.)

CHAPTER VIII

Bible Stories: Stories of Jesus

No portion of the Bible has been so continuously used by storytellers of all types as the Gospels. Single stories, whole series of imaginary tales, and even full-length novels, purely fictional, have grown out of an author's interpretation of an act or a teaching of Jesus. Radio dramas, plays, and feature motion pictures have tried to reproduce his life and times, and dramatize with imagined or historic detail the effect of his life on others. Fulton Oursler's series, *The Greatest Story Ever Told*, gives examples of stories frankly imaginary but in which we see principles laid down by Jesus at work in the lives of persons who heard him teach. A short story of this type, useful in children's departments, is Truman Douglass' " The Second Mile " (see Appendix).

Many of our " lesson stories " have fallen far short of good story standards, have not, in fact, been stories at all. Jesus' walk on the hillside one day, for instance, where he was followed by crowds to whom he voiced a " saying " does not make a story — unless the " saying " is an answer to a problem indicated at the beginning, and comes as a climax to questions or struggles of someone in the crowd in whom we are interested.

Expanding the stories to make the characters stand out and inviting identification with them calls for imagination, but leaders have a special obligation in their use of it in developing incidents from the life of Jesus.

We Must Be True to the Spirit of the Basic Material

We must put the emphasis in the right place. If we are telling one of the miracle stories we shall not focus on details of the miracle in such a way as to make it seem like magic, and Jesus an almost magical wonder-worker. That would not be keeping true to the spirit of Jesus. Our emphasis will be on the person's need, and Jesus' ability, through Love's eyes, to see what the need really was and to meet it. Or it will be on the effect his acts had on those who witnessed them. Our imaginations can be directed towards details of the plight of the persons involved, or the situation which Jesus was trying to better. In a " healing " story we can imagine the invalid's helplessness, feel his pain, his discouragement, his lack of faith in ever being better, his awareness, on meeting Jesus, that here was a friend who understood him and knew exactly how to help him. In our imagination we can feel with him what is really wrong, and want it to be made right. We can almost feel that power that is coming through Jesus to cure him. That kind of imagination does not do violence to the spirit of the text, though it leaves the text far behind at times.

We Should also Be True to Fact

Background material should be correct as to time, locale, conditions, and customs. Books listed in the Bibliography will give this type of information. Note the care which Margaret Dulles Edwards has taken to study the background for the story of the Widow's Mites (see " Thank Offerings " in Appendix) and to present this to her listeners (juniors).

Our mental pictures of characters and events in the Bible have been colored by paintings, poetry, and traditions with which we have grown up. Without visiting the Bible lands themselves or having the benefit of photographs of them, the early artists of Italy, Germany, France, and Spain painted their masterpieces as their imaginations (and their countryside, their customs, their models) suggested that the scenes might look. Storytellers have patterned their own images after these pictures, regardless of the fact that manners and customs of the West differ from those of the East.

The status of the Near East woman, for instance, has not been such that she would be favored as she is in the West. The Palestinian woman serves her menfolk first, before she herself eats. She is more likely to lead the donkey than ride on his back, which is reserved for burdens, though a man may ride while the woman walks ahead. Little boys at quite an early age follow their father's occupation, not their mother's. Men's work is in the shop, the market, and the fields. Women concern themselves with household tasks. Boys would not carry water from the well, ordinarily. That is women's work. Their customs may not be ours, but we are telling their stories, not ours.

We tend to sentimentalize the fact that "there was no room at the inn," emphasizing the fact to suit our purpose, and not realizing that there were no such things as "private rooms and baths" in the Eastern khan. A typical "inn" might have two rooms, one for the family's living and the other for the travelers' sleeping. A mat, unrolled on the floor, accommodated each guest inside the house, but such luxury was for the well-to-do. A wall-enclosed courtyard, in a mild climate, with the possibility of a sheltering roof in one corner, was acceptable and usual for caravans and humble folk, who were used to sleeping with their animals.

Books, photographs, Bible dictionaries, and returned travelers can help us to use accurate details.

Characters Should Be True to Type. A Palestine fisherman should be a Palestine fisherman. If the story is going into detail, he must seine his fish, clean and mend his nets, cook his meals on the shore, as Palestine fishermen do and have done for centuries.

Personalities should speak and act according to their characteristics as shown in the records. We should avoid attributing traits and attitudes to them for which there is no foundation, else the children, reading the stories for themselves, will be bewildered and distrustful of all we have given them.

Vocabulary. Words change their meanings. In telling stories we have to consider the associations children have with words, and how quickly prejudices can be formed. In telling " The Good Samaritan," for instance, a danger can be avoided by substituting for the word " priest " something like " a man who worked in the big temple in the city," or by explaining that the priest in the story was not like the priests the children may know today. Similarly, we should not use such a phrase as " the Jews killed Jesus " any more than we should, in telling of an incident in our own history, say " The Americans killed Abraham Lincoln."

On the other hand the use of too modern terms is also out of place. Substituting " gangsters " for robbers in the story of the Good Samaritan is an example. This was a story which Jesus told, not one you are telling as an actual happening, and the modern term would lift it out of its setting.

THE PARABLES OF JESUS

The use of parables was a favorite form of teaching with Jesus. He taught his lessons imaginatively, as creative teachers do. It is as if they asked themselves, " How can I dramatize this truth to make it clear? " But Jesus was talking to adults capable of seeing comparisons and implications for their own living, or of finding the kernel of the truth to which his story pointed.

As discussed in Chapter III, little children do not see these similarities. Older boys and girls and young people can see the spread of an idea — or the kingdom of Heaven — in the story of the Mustard Seed, but its value as a Bible story in its symbolic meaning is lost to six-year-olds.

The parable of the Sower would be a mere statement of facts to younger children and probably not very interesting ones, at that. But consider an adult group listening to a presentation of Jesus as an optimist and hearing the familiar parable. What new significance is given the term as they now see Jesus " not as an optimist thinking all's right with the world, but facing a world where three-fourths of the seed came to nothing — and wagering his life on the one-fourth that fell on the good ground."

The allusion to the Good Shepherd who leaves the ninety and nine to go after the lost sheep is not a story at all, but suggests one, and is often expanded into a story and offered as one told by Jesus. Even so, told to little children, it would not mean what Jesus meant. Divine concern over the " lost " which Jesus was constantly demonstrating in his life is better illustrated for the younger children by any one of the incidents in which he brought back to usefulness and self-respect one who had lost both. References to such incidents will be found at the end of this chapter.

Different Purposes for Different Groups

Stories of Jesus are chosen for different purposes for different listeners. The age and experience of one's group determine the emphasis and climax.

To little children acts of kindness and helpfulness in great need make good introductions to Jesus. (Repetition of such stories through the years, however, with no change in approach or purpose, exhausts interest in him by the time he should be making his greatest appeal.)

Stories to show the difference he made in people's lives, through concern for their problems, furnish an approach for older primary children. They can see things happen in their own experience when his spirit of friendliness is at work.

For juniors and older boys and girls, who are looking for heroes, to present him against a background of ignorance, superstition, traditional formalism, and hostility which constantly threatened his safety emphasizes his courage and makes a strong appeal.

To young people and adults a story of Jesus should carry a challenge to complacency and accepted worldly standards. It should invite the testing of one's own standards and activities by ideals which are truly Christian.

Putting Yourself into the Story

A story given in your text may be well written and vivid, and suited to the needs of your group. But it needs more before you can tell it effectively. You must put yourself into the story, your imagination and your emotions. You need to understand the feelings of the characters, to know what made them act as they did. You must see the setting.

This is the exciting part of your preparation. Your feelings, of course, should be backed up by everything you can find which throws light on the story. Background material is probably included in your textbook. You read it carefully, and then go to the Bible for the original story.

Using a Harmony of the Gospels. The more you read, the more you begin to feel. Is there more than one version of this same story? This is where a *Harmony of the Gospels* makes fascinating reading, as you see the same incident in parallel columns. You note the swift action in Mark, as though the events had just happened, although at least thirty years had elapsed since Jesus had died. The precious recollections were vividly set down to reinspire and instruct the hunted and persecuted Christians in Rome.

Matthew had another reason for writing a decade later, and another audience, as did Luke, a few years after Matthew, and last of all, two generations after Jesus died, John, interpreting for Greek believers the meaning of the Christian gospel. But all three used Mark's account as their chief source, sometimes duplicating a story, sometimes telling it differently, as it passed into other tongues. Thus it is a good plan, in working up a feeling for your story, to read all accounts. Sometimes, of course, each writer added, from the growing store of recollections of the Master, incidents and teachings not recorded elsewhere.

Different Translations of the Bible. If your church school or your private library has the *Moffatt, Goodspeed, Weymouth,* and Revised Standard versions of the New Testament, you will find your visualization easier and more accurate in little details of your story as you look up the accounts in the various versions. The paralytic let down through the roof, for instance, will be found to be on a "bed," a "couch," a "pallet," and a "mat." Which would make the story easier for your listeners to visualize, as the paralytic takes it up and walks off?

Why Four Men Tore Up a Roof

Since we mention this story, let us consider the points from which different teachers make a selection, according to the age of the children who will hear it. (See Matt. 9: 2-8; Mark 2: 1-12; Luke 5: 17-26)

Place: Capernaum.

Time: "One of those days that he was teaching."

Situation: Jesus inside a house where so many were gathered together — scribes and Pharisees among them — no more room.

Men came, carrying a man sick of the palsy on a bed; tried to enter, crowd too great; carried him to roof. (Look up pictures of Eastern houses.)

Jesus, *seeing their faith* (teacher notes this phrase: it is in each of the versions), said, " Your sins are forgiven."

Scribes charge blasphemy, Jesus answers, bids paralytic rise. He is cured; friends' faith justified.

From whose point of view would you tell this story — the Four Friends'? The Paralytic's? The Disciples'? The Scribes'? The Narrator's?

For primary children the interest will be in the efforts of the sick man's friends to get him to someone they were sure would help him. (How do we know they were sure? Because of those important words, " Jesus, seeing their faith." Evidently their faith had a great deal to do with the cure.) The cure, of course, is the climax.

From the friends' point of view, the story will elaborate on how they felt about their friend and his illness. Older primary children will feel sad to think he could only lie there, remembering all he had done and all he wished he hadn't done before he was ill, and wishing he could be well and start over again. (These guilt feelings must have been worrying him or Jesus would not have put his finger on them, clearing them away before the physical cure took place. If the cure depended on forgiveness, early reference must be made to the guilt. For younger primary children it would not be brought in. Emphasis would be on the friends' helpfulness.)

The storyteller would go on to imagine how they heard of Jesus and his healings, and immediately thought of their paralyzed friend; with what hope and eagerness they got his consent to let them carry him to Jesus (details here, each one having a suggestion; direct discourse); how they started out; what they saw as they neared the house; what they said. (This is the place for suspense. Make the project look hopeless.) Even after one suggests going up to the roof, would it be safe? Could they manage the outside steps, not too wide? What if one of them let a corner drop? The friend could not help himself. They knew how roofs were built, with beams and mud plaster tiles. Could they manage to untile a large enough place between the beams to let their friend down? Could they do it safely? And how could they find a clear space in front of Jesus, with the people crowding around him?

There is nothing to do but try and keep on believing that things will come out right. They put the mat in a shady place near the low wall around the roof and go to work. As the hole grows larger, one tile after another being lifted off, and they look down into the crowded room, they see the people below looking up wonderingly at them. They have a chance to explain. As they gently lower their friend, they see the crowd in front of Jesus push back. Jesus looks from them to the sick man and back to them again. What is he thinking, they wonder. Will he help? He *must*, they have been to such pains to bring their friend here; have been so sure that whatever is wrong with him Jesus can make right.

Jesus' look gives them new hope. It is as if he were saying to them, " I can see how you believe I can help him. And so I can."

They hardly move as they watch him. Even the crowd is quiet. He looks down at the sick man and there is kindness in his voice as he calls him " Son," and strength as he tells him to have courage, that whatever mistakes he has made are forgiven.

The friends are surprised. They had thought Jesus would heal their friend's sickness. That was why they had brought him here. The people below are surprised, too. The men on the roof hear them murmuring. What did it mean? Did Jesus care more about the mistakes the man had made and about setting them right? He must have known they had worried the sick man. Maybe it was more important to both of them than the sickness itself. But what was this he was saying now? And what did the four friends see as they looked down?

" Get up," Jesus was saying. " Take up your mat and go home." And their friend was getting up! He was rolling up his mat. He was looking at Jesus, then up at his friends with a new look on his face! Everything his friends had wished for him, and more, had happened! They hurried to put back the tiles, almost singing in their hearts, " We knew if we brought him to Jesus he could help; we knew! We knew! "

Thus the storyteller sees and feels her story. Thus she sketches in her sequences, remembering the age of her audience, putting in only those details which will make the climax most dramatic, taking care that the climax answers the anticipation aroused at the beginning, and remembering always from whose point of view she is telling her story.

THE MAN AT THE POOL OF BETHESDA

Let us listen in on a storytelling class which is considering these problems. It may give us ideas. The assignment on the board reads: *Retell the story of the Man at the Pool of Bethesda. John 5: 1-18.*

Teacher: Who is ready with the story?

1st Student: I am, Miss ————. One Sabbath day at the Pool of Bethesda Jesus saw a man who had been sick thirty-eight years. He was waiting for the water to bubble up, so he could be the first one to drop in and be healed. Someone was always ahead of him. Jesus saw him and healed him.

Teacher: Comments?

2d Student: I shouldn't call that a story.

Teacher: Why not?

2d Student: It's just a string of statements.

3d Student: He hasn't given any background for the invalid's being there.

4th Student: Nor any details to make the pictures clear.

5th Student: There was no attempt to gain any sympathy for the invalid.

6th Student: Or any interest in the personality or the concerns of Jesus.

7th Student: There was no working up to a climax.

Teacher: What is the climax, and what details would you suggest?

8th Student: It would depend on my audience and the point I wanted to make.

Teacher: Can you show how these would vary with your listeners?

8th Student: Well, I teach little children. My purpose would be to illustrate the kindness and helpfulness of Jesus; show him bringing new joy and usefulness to one who had lost both. My climax would come when he gives the man power to walk. I'd tell the story from the point of view of the "infirm man" and I'd build up sympathy through details. He couldn't dress himself; couldn't go out to walk; couldn't go to his friends' parties. He'd been sick for thirty-eight years! He'd tried all sorts of "cures." For a long time now he'd been coming to this pool. (I'd tell about the bubbling up, and people's belief about it.) I'd make it hard for him to get there, and harder to get himself into the pool first of the bathers. He was sure the pool would cure him but there was disappointment after disappointment. Couldn't he *ever* be cured? Just then I'd have him see Jesus, and after that — the climax. "The Sabbath" wouldn't enter in for the younger ones.

9th Student: I teach older children. I'd tell that story to show how Jesus could make people believe in themselves — in their own capacities, in the Spirit of God in them. I'd imagine the steps that made the man lose faith in himself and depend on the magic of the pool. Jesus comes, sees the man's real need, for he asks, "Do you *want* to be well?" (I always thought the man's answer was an evasion of the issue.) My climax would come with Jesus' persuading the man to try powers he had never used, perhaps never suspected.

Teacher: Any other approaches?

10th Student: Yes, Miss ————, the Sabbath-breaking one, — that was important, you know. I have junior high boys and girls. I want them to see the emphasis Jesus placed on people *versus* laws. I'd like to imagine what effect his act would have on a sensitive, law-abiding Jew who might be troubled because the law forbade him to give help to a friend who needed him. That help would be violating the Sabbath law prohibiting any form of "work." (I'd have to go into that a little, to show that the sick man's carrying his bed was a violation, and Jesus' curing his infirmity.) I'd have the law-abiding Jew happen to visit the pool, and see the cure. He'd be indignant and resentful, along with other law-abiding persons, then he would see the *sense* in Jesus' attitude. Of course my details would emphasize his friend's need and the laws restricting him. The climax would come when he rushed back to the aid of his friend with new understanding of Jesus' law of love.

Teacher: Three possible approaches. In each instance, how would you prepare yourself to make the story as vivid and as true to the background as possible?

1st Student: Read it several times.

2d Student: See if and how another Gospel tells the story.

3d Student: Read commentaries.

Teacher: On what?

4th Student: On beliefs about the pool.

9th Student: On the sick man's "infirmity."

10th Student: On the laws of the Sabbath.

11th Student: Yes, and in connection with that, I'd look up other incidents of Jesus healing on the Sabbath, and find what he said about laws that prevented people from living the good life.

Teacher: And having learned all you can, will you put all your new findings into your story?

Chorus: No! Only those which advance the story towards its climax.

Teacher: Good. You can't have too much background, but don't use it wastefully. Class dismissed.

Assignments for Story Workshop

1. After listening to the storytelling (assigned last week) and participating in it, let the class turn to the discussion of background material for stories on pages 86, 87 and select an episode which they as a group wish to expand into a story for third- or fourth-grade children.

2. Let someone with a *Harmony* find out if different Gospels have recorded the incident, and read each account to the class. (See Bibliography for titles of a *Harmony of the Gospels* and books for later assignments.)

3. In the same way let those who have brought different versions of the Bible read them.

4. Other members of the class may read from Commentary or Bible Dictionary information in regard to customs, laws, descriptions of localities, interpretations, etc., needed to give realism to the story.

5. Now, as a class, decide on a climax, then on a good beginning for the story, then on action and suspense elements, and finally on a good ending.

6. Students should be taking notes of the steps outlined and any background information they can use to make the story "come alive." For next week each student should prepare the story for telling.

BIBLE REFERENCES FOR STORY BACKGROUNDS
WHICH SHOW JESUS' ATTITUDES
TOWARDS PERSONS AND PRACTICES

Teachers will realize that the references are not to stories to be told to children, although of course many are suitable. The references are given rather for background information for teachers of any age-group, to give a true picture of Jesus as a person and as an interpreter of the nature and will of God.

Concern for the crowds, the sick, and the handicapped

" When he saw the multitudes, he was moved with compassion for them."
    Matt. 9: 36-38
Heals Simon's wife's mother. Mark 1: 30, 31
Man at the pool of Bethesda. John 5: 1-9
"At even, when the sun did set." Mark 1: 32-34
Cleanses a leper. Mark 1: 40-42
Ten lepers. Luke 17: 11-19
Man sick of the palsy. Mark 2: 1-12
Many people came to be healed. Luke 6: 17-19
Casts out an unclean spirit. Mark 1: 23-28
The Gerasene demoniac. Mark 5: 1-20
The blind and dumb. Matt. 9: 27-34
The deaf and dumb. Mark 7: 32-37
Blind man of Bethsaida. Mark 8: 22-26
Blind Bartimaeus. Mark 10: 46-52
Boy with a dumb spirit. Mark 9: 14-29

Attitude towards sinners and outcasts

Matthew, tax collector, called. Mark 2: 14
Sits at meat with publicans. Mark 2: 15-17
Goes to home of Zacchaeus, tax collector. Luke 19: 1-10
A woman with alabaster cruse. Mark 14: 3-9; Luke 7: 36-50
" It is not the will of your Father . . . that one of these little ones should perish." Matt. 18: 14

Consideration of women

Samaritan woman at Jacob's well. John 4: 4-39
Adulterous woman accused. John 7: 53—8: 11
Woman with alabaster cruse. Mark 14: 3-9; Luke 7: 36-50; John 12: 1-8
Poor widow with two mites. Mark 12: 41-44

Consideration of children

Blesses little children. Mark 10: 13-16
"A little child . . . in the midst." Matt. 18: 2-4; Mark 9: 36, 37
Acknowledges children's praise in the temple. Matt. 21: 15, 16

Emphasis on importance of persons vs. laws

Sabbath day laws. (See Exod. 20: 8-11; Numbers 15: 32-36.)
Disciples in grainfields. Mark 2: 23-28; Matt. 12: 1-8; Luke 6: 1-5
Man with withered hand. Matt. 12: 9-14; Mark 3: 1-6; Luke 6: 6-11
Woman with infirmity. Luke 13: 10-16
Man at the pool of Bethesda. John 5: 1-18
A blind man. John 9: 1-16
Man with dropsy. Luke 14: 1-5

Standards of righteousness (*Background for stories of contrasts between generally accepted ideas and those of Jesus*)

"Except your righteousness shall exceed . . . the scribes and Pharisees." Matt. 5: 20
"Ye have heard that it was said . . . but I say." (Anger) Matt. 5: 21-29
"An eye for an eye . . . Resist not him that is evil;" The second mile. Matt. 5: 38-42
"Love your enemies." Matt. 5: 43, 44
The Golden Rule. Matt. 7: 12; Luke 6: 31
"If ye love them that love you, what reward have ye? " Matt. 5: 46, 47; Luke 6: 32-35
"Seek ye first." Matt. 6: 33
Righteousness to be seen of men. Matt. 6: 1-18
The mote and the beam. Matt. 7: 3
Forgiveness, seventy times seven. Matt. 18: 21, 22
The prodigal son. Luke 15: 11-32
Forgiving trespasses. Matt. 6: 14
"Fire from heaven," inhospitable Samaritans. Luke 9: 51-56

Religious practices (*More contrasts*)

Mercy, not sacrifice. Matt. 12: 1-8
Pray not as the hypocrites. Matt. 6: 5-8
"Not every one that saith . . . Lord, Lord." Matt. 7: 21
"Two men went up into the temple to pray." Luke 18: 9-14
The Lord's Prayer. Matt. 6: 9-13
Jesus spends night in prayer. Luke 6: 12-19
Disciples find Jesus in prayer. Mark 1: 35-38
Almsgiving, the widow's mites. Mark 12: 41-44
"Your Father knoweth what things ye have need of, before ye ask him." Matt. 6: 8

Standards of greatness

James and John want honors. Mark 10: 35-37; 41-45
Jesus washes the disciples' feet. John 13: 1-15

Denunciation of scribes and Pharisees (Background for stories showing insincerity and cruelty caused by wrong ideas of what is important)

Heavy burdens put upon people. Matt. 23: 1-4; Luke 11: 46
" Who desire to walk in long robes, and to have salutations . . . and chief seats in the synagogues." Matt. 23: 2-7; Mark 12: 38-40; Luke 20: 45-47
Alms and tithing; strain out the gnat and swallow the camel; cleanse the outside of the cup and platter. Matt. 23: 23-26; Luke 11: 39-42
Value of a gift, the widow's mites. Mark 12: 41-44
Cleanliness and real defilement. Mark 7: 1-23; Matt. 15: 18-20
True values, " not in the abundance of the things which he possesseth." Luke 12: 13-15

Home relationships of Jesus

" Subject " to parents. Luke 2: 51, 52
Elder brother in home. Matt. 13: 55, 56; Mark 6: 3
Family attitude towards Jesus. John 7: 2-5

Jesus' fame; opinions of the populace; enmity (Background for stories showing how Jesus continued his work in spite of danger)

" He taught them as having authority, and not as the scribes." Mark 1: 21, 22
His fame. Matt. 4: 24, 25; Mark 6: 53-56
Needs a boat because of the crowd. Mark 3: 7-12
Friends' opinion, " He is beside himself." Mark 3: 19-21
His " way " hard, many went back. John 6: 43-66
Opinion of his family. John 7: 2-5
Opinion of the populace. John 7: 10-13, 25-27
" For power came forth from him." Luke 6: 17-19
Procession on Palm Sunday. Mark 11: 1-11
Scribes criticize healing, " Who can forgive sins but one, even God? " Mark 2: 1-12
Enmity aroused. Matt. 21: 15, 16; Mark 3: 6; 12: 12; Luke 11: 53, 54; 13: 31, 32; 19: 47; 20: 19
Attempt to get evidence against Jesus. Mark 12: 13-34
Jesus cleanses the temple. Mark 11: 15-19; John 2: 13-16

Jesus' own idea of his mission; of God; of one's duty towards his neighbor

Sabbath preaching at Nazareth. Luke 4: 16-30 (Prophecy from Isaiah 61: 1, 2)
" Fishers of men." Mark 1: 16-20; Matt. 4: 18-22; Luke 5: 1-11

Communion with his Father. Mark 1: 35-39
" To this end came I forth." Mark 1: 38, 39
" Your heavenly Father knoweth." Matt. 6: 25-34
The good shepherd. Luke 15: 3-7
The lost coin. Luke 15: 8-10
" Love one another." John 13: 34, 35
Parable of the forgiving father. Luke 15: 11-32
Parable of the good Samaritan. Luke 10: 29-37
Parable of the talents. Luke 19: 11-26; Matt. 25: 14-29
" God is spirit." John 4: 24 (R.S.V.)

Stories from the Book of The Acts showing Jesus' continuing spirit

Of community living and sharing. Acts 2: 44-47
Barnabas sells his lands. Acts 4: 34-37
Peter and John at the Gate Beautiful. Acts 3: 1-10

Parables on the kingdom of heaven

Wheat and tares; mustard seed; leaven; hidden treasure; pearl of great
    price. Matt. 13

Key passages

" Greater works than these shall he do." John 14: 12
" If ye love me, ye will keep my commandments." John 14: 15
" God is spirit: and those who worship him must worship in spirit and
    truth." John 4: 24 (R.S.V.)
" Thou shalt love the Lord thy God with all thy heart, and with all thy
    soul, and with all thy mind, and with all thy strength." Mark 12: 30
    (Deut. 6: 5)
" Thou shalt love thy neighbor as thyself." Mark 12: 31 (See also Leviticus
    19: 18)
The Sermon on the Mount: the Beatitudes; the Lord's Prayer; the Golden
    Rule. Matt. 5, 6, 7

CHAPTER IX

True Stories from Different Sources

" Is it true? " is the question a children's storyteller hears most frequently. If the answer is " Yes," she senses the satisfaction with which her young listeners settle back. Storytellers for any age over six or seven will be wise if they make the most of biography, drama in the mission field, and accounts of everyday heroism frequently observed or found in the daily news.

BIOGRAPHY — SINGLE STORIES OR SERIALS?

We have already indicated the importance of and uses for the biographical story. (See chapters III and IV.) In a chapter on true stories it must be mentioned again for its special place in religious education, and for the organization of material to make it effective for our use.

In presenting a true story of a life our aim is to show the spirit of that life in such a way as to affect the spirit of other lives.

The story may be told in one of three ways: (1) making the climax of the hero's career the culmination of several episodes, through his life, all of which can be recounted in one storytelling period; or (2) telling the story serially, making a complete story of each episode; or (3) selecting one incident or period in his life which typifies his spirit, and working that into a story with its own climax.

For younger listeners (2) and (3) are by far the most satisfactory. Stories which cover a long span of time lose in effect. A character will stand out more vividly through one episode, or series of episodes covering one period of time, than through many, colorful though they may be, but having years of time between them. Therefore what is left out is almost as important as what is left in. Always we are striving for unity with one end in view, one kind of feeling to be aroused.

Another argument in favor of telling a biographical story serially is that the tone of a life changes through the years. A boy starts out in life often with a different aim from the one with which he ends. Can the storyteller so organize her facts as to recognize this and yet keep the story moving forward?

Elizabeth Reed commences a story introducing the life of St. Francis: " Once there was a boy who wanted to be a prince." A beguiling introduction: the hero wants something. *Will he get it?* the radio announcer would anxiously ask. That is what the author wants us to ask. We think he is on his way, at the climax of the first installment, when he is chosen by his gay companions to lead their carnival procession in princely clothes and on his father's white horse.

But that is only one story. There have been dramatic moments of suspense in this, when the spirit of his princely objective was challenged by the beggar who came to him " in the name of God " and was thrust out, and then followed and brought back, to the disgust of Francis' friends.

Another story or two, each with its own struggle between two ways of life, leads to his great climactic decision. After stormy opposition from his father and worldly friends, he renounces all connection with the life they represent to travel the way of humble service, the way in which Jesus led him. The final climax may seem to fail in answering the anticipation aroused at the beginning when Francis voluntarily (and dramatically) casts off his princely clothes to change to the role of Brother. But if the listeners have identified themselves from the first with Francis, they will have grown along with him. As they themselves have recognized higher goals, they will welcome his final decision, for new anticipations have been aroused.

THE NEWSPAPER A SOURCE FOR TRUE STORIES

Many a news item can be worked into a hero or adventure tale by observing the " rules " of this story game.

The daily paper has arrived. We turn to the pages most likely to have the " human interest " items. Our eyes are held by a headline. *Something has happened to someone!*

That is usually the climax. We can in imagination supply the steps to this climax even though details are sparse. If we are interested at all in the event, there must be a story behind it that can make hearers eager to know how it could have happened. Read through the item and see what help the reporter has given you. Perhaps he has provided you with the entire story. Perhaps the headlines are enough to start your imagination.

Look down this list of authentic headlines and see their possibilities. Then follow the rules suggested in chapters II and V and make your own story!

HEADLINES

(1) 100 BOYS REPAY DOCTOR'S AID TO CHUM
They Polish His Car, Then Clean the Sidewalk and Office Door to Say " Thank You."

(2) COLLIE, GOING BLIND, GETS SEEING-EYE DACHSHUND

(3) BOY WINS VACATION – GIVES IT TO FRIEND
Says Younger Lad, Underweight, Needs Trip to Camp More Than He Does.

(4) BOSTON LAWYER DEAD; SET UP NEWSBOY FUND
Helped Children with Problems He Had as an Immigrant.

(5) DOG GETS MEDAL FOR SAVING LIFE OF SERVICE MAN
A. S. P. C. A. Honors Pat for Finding Coast Guardsman Who Fainted.

(6) PASSENGERS TILT SUBWAY CAR, FREE WOMAN
Alert Change Agent Lines 150 Along Platform; One Big Push Releases Her.

(7) JOHN CLIMBS TREE TO RETRIEVE AIRPLANE, CAN'T GET DOWN
Firemen with Extension Ladder Rescue Boy from Precarious Treetop Perch.

True Stories from the Mission Field [1]

The mission field has always been an unlimited source for stories. It is today, though the work of the missionary has somewhat changed, due in part to the missionary enterprise itself. Trained indigenous leadership has developed, manning schools and hospitals, once entirely staffed by foreigners, with nationals — native leaders. In many places the missionary's work is now institutional, his talents being used in organizing or supervising. His direct contact with the people is lessened. Also our concept of missionary work has broadened. It now means feeding hungry people on a large scale, introducing more productive farming methods. It means preventing sickness, as well as curing it, introducing sanitation methods and health education. It means producing and spreading literacy among the villages independent of the mission schools. It requires skills of all kinds and the consecrated Christian who in former days went out to preach the gospel of Love now goes out to demonstrate it. In his work and his relationships he is often reflecting the spirit of Christ, before he tells his story in words.

These changes, along with the fact that we are all nearer to each other than we have ever been, more likely to meet, more dependent on each other, should make our missionary stories for high school and young people more vivid and challenging than ever before.

---

[1] See also the discussion of missionary stories in Chapter IV.

Surely one of our aims in telling missionary stories to children is to help them understand people of other groups; to present them as persons like ourselves, with the same physical make-up as ourselves, with the same yearnings, the same responses to beauty and love; activated by the same motives as ourselves. *We are children of one Father.* Let us in our stories feel this, making the story children so closely related to our listeners that they will see no difference between these children and themselves.

We copied this from an English missionary story as an illustration of a good "Topical Beginning." We give it now as a good beginning for a children's missionary story:

It was the most exciting thing that had ever happened, Prem thought, as he jumped down from the creaking bullock cart. [There follow a few sentences, sketching in the Indian village.] All his life Prem had wanted to see the real jungle. [And the storyteller plunges into her story.][2]

Can you imagine a primary child not wanting to follow Prem into the jungle? Or not understanding his excitement?

ASSIGNMENTS FOR STORY WORKSHOP

Every member of a storytelling class should have the opportunity to tell at least one story before the class. One grows in confidence with such "public" practice.

Assignments previously given have been, of course, only suggestions. There are so many types of stories used in religious education that students will have a choice in this "practice storytelling" between those mentioned in the last four chapters.

[2] From a story by Mary Entwistle.

CHAPTER X

Stories for Appreciation

APPRECIATION OF WORSHIP

We all recognize the value of the story in the service of worship. It can of itself create an atmosphere and the mood for worship. It can even explain the function of the act or of the service of worship. A story like " Maisie's First Meeting " in *The Children's Story Garden* does a part of this for primary children, at the beginning of the year. The stories " Be Still . . . and Know That I Am God " and " The Still, Small Voice " may do it for older boys and girls (see Appendix).

A " Service of Worthship." A discussion of what is meant when one says " That is worth a great deal " will usually reveal the children's understanding of worth to be in terms of money. Stories which lead them to value a friendship, an act of heroism, loyalty, or unselfishness above goods purchasable in a department store, and which give them a standard for measuring spiritual against material values are also helping them to understand why " worthship " is the origin of " worship."

APPRECIATION OF A PARTICULAR FACET OF LIFE

Some collections have stories which, because they do not follow the " story " pattern, are difficult to tell with effect. They are better read than told, for there is more conversation than movement, more " moral teaching " than plot. Often they are brief, with no invitation to identify oneself emotionally with the hero and no sense of achievement or satisfaction at the end.

Their purpose, however, is not the unfolding of a drama, but the focusing on an aspect of life which may induce wonder, a desire for more knowledge, or a new awareness of a great universal truth. This focus may be just what a leader desires for a service of worship or to add significance to a class experience. She will therefore study to find how to make the most effective use of such stories. Good examples are found in " The Fig Seed," "A Musician and His Trumpet," " The Lump of Salt," and other stories in the story collection *From Long Ago and Many Lands* by Sophia L. Fahs.

Appreciation of the One-ness of Humanity

We are constantly in need of stories in the worship service and in class discussion which get behind and beyond prejudices and which show us all as children of *one God*, each with likable traits, each with strengths, insights, and abilities which, put together, can bring stability and harmony to this world.

" Nathan's Friend " and " The Second Mile " (see Appendix) are illustrations of such stories on the primary and junior level.

A favorite, good all the way from older primary to junior high school age, is Raymond Macdonald Alden's " The Palace Made by Music " in *Why the Chimes Rang and Other Stories*. This story has several times been the springboard for a real experience of different groups or individuals coming together with their particular contributions, to demonstrate the beauty of harmonious co-operation.

Another story based on harmony, " The Heavenly Music " (see Appendix), symbolizes quaintly for adults the state of a world where each section claims for itself a monopoly of the truth — and where there is no sharing of what each has found. The old German folk tale was introduced to us in one of Dr. St. John's storytelling classes. It is interesting to the storyteller who tries to analyze its construction, for he must look to a far distant future for its climax. It is a tender fantasy, however, and has power to send its message home more surely than the literal truth to which we will not listen.

APPRECIATION OF MUSIC

The power of music to soothe a disturbed spirit and cure a sick mind has been known for centuries. Gratitude for it and for those gifted and skilled in the ability to use this power in healing ways might, a primary leader once thought, lead to a new attitude towards music practice. It also might set a new keynote to the department's annual music service. At this service any child playing a musical instrument could take part. As the juvenile skill ranged all the way from "one hand" tunes to quite advanced pieces, it was sometimes difficult to keep it from becoming a "recital" with attention placed on performance.

If the focus could be the opportunity which music-makers have to bring beauty and joy and content to their listeners, then each child's contribution could be seen as the particular step in his progress towards this end. The right story would emphasize the desirable values.

The combination of an article on the therapeutic use of music in modern mental hospitals, of Browning's "Saul," and of 1 Samuel 16: 14-23, gave the leader the inspiration for her story in which Saul's despondency was described (with details suggested by all three sources) and Jesse's sending of his shepherd son with his lyre to Jerusalem, laden with gifts for the king. Browning's poem makes one fairly hear the music which gradually aroused Saul from his lethargy. One can see the white sheep, the long grasses by the stream, the stars coming out one by one, as the lines bring them before one. There was a storyteller! The leader could draw freely on the poet's imagery until her story came to an end with: "But of all the gifts David brought to the palace that day, none was so great as his gift of music which had helped him bring back to health and joy a sick and troubled king."

The playing by a neighboring professional harpist of a nature composition, which might have been like David's own, lifted the group to a level where with sincerity they could say, "Thank you, God, for music, and for those who bring it to us! "

Composers and Hymns. Stories of composers and their music give added meaning and listening pleasure to the compositions whenever they are heard. Hymn stories enrich worship and furnish associations which make them doubly appreciated. There are numerous hymn-story collections but the accounts are often too brief to be dramatized. This is an excellent field in which to let loose our imagination.

The writer remembers a dramatic moment in a service of a junior department she chanced to share one morning. The Watts hymn, whose author and date of composition had been noted as it was announced, was " O God, Our Help in Ages Past." It was just finished when the door at the back of the room opened and a man's voice thundered forth, " Stop! In the name of the law, I command that these proceedings be stopped!" As he was shouting his command, a big six-footer stalked past the wide-eyed children to the platform and placed a heavy hand on the leader. Shrinking from his touch she backed away, asking weakly, " What do you mean? "

" I mean this is not allowed — what you are doing here — you are breaking the law. You're to come with me."

" But we've been doing this right along! " she protested; " what is wrong about it? "

" You'll find out soon enough. You are all under arrest. Come on, men! " (Waving towards the door)

By this time, of course, children and teachers alike were transfixed in their chairs. In fact, the illusion was so perfect that even though the " officer of the law " was one of the popular teachers in the department, dressed as usual, no one seemed to know quite what to think, even after the two on the platform stepped out of their roles.

When the atmosphere was a bit more relaxed and the children could laugh a little sheepishly at themselves, the leader introduced her story: " But that's exactly what happened to Isaac Watts's father when little Isaac was only two years old. . . ."

This was one of a series of services during which the leader was introducing the juniors to a part of their religious heritage, making them aware of some of the struggles and sacrifices endured. We are quite sure they will not forget it!

Appreciation of Art

Great paintings have their stories, or suggest them. Pictures like Millet's " The Angelus " and Breton's " Song of the Lark " are aids to worship, and, like pieces of music, if dramatized by storytelling, become fixed with association.

Many leaders have used a popular story of Albrecht Dürer's " Praying Hands " effectively with a reproduction of his picture, though the story has no basis of fact. Legends about a person or his work should be told as legends, and may be quite as useful in arousing responses; facts about famous persons can always be found in libraries.

A story we like to tell after showing and discussing Taylor's picture, " When I Consider Thy Heavens," is " The Constant Star " (see Appendix).

Appreciation of the Constant in the Universe

Teachers looking for stories which illustrate the dependability of nature's laws will find others besides " The Constant Star " in Alice Geer Kelsey's book, *Stories for Junior Worship*. The migration of the birds tells the same tale: the reliability of the sun for telling time. Such stories not only inspire wonder and litanies of thanksgiving, but help to give children the feeling of security in a world full of surprises.

STORIES THAT ARE NOT TRUE

In answer to a child's query, "Is it true?" we may say, "No, but it's a 'true-to-life' story." Children evidently understand this term for a realistic narrative.

Or we may say, "No, but there is something true about it. See if you can find out what it is." A story like "The Palace Made by Music" brings forth, "The earthquake could be true"; "But the palace disappearing like that and coming back — that couldn't be true." "But it's true that lots of people playing together make prettier music than just one playing by himself."

Or we may say of a myth, "No, but once people believed it was true," or of a legend, "Perhaps not, but ————— was such a famous ————— that all sorts of stories grew up about him, and this was one of the favorites."

Or of the purely humorous bit of fiction we might say, "Of course it couldn't be true, but the one who wrote it thought it would amuse us."

All humorous stories are not funny to all ages. One like the Japanese folk tale of the boy with the name of Tiki-tiki-tembo-no-so-rembo-ara-bara-buski-ip-eri-pendo-hyki-pon-pon-nichi-no-meono-don-bianco (see Appendix) will send boys and girls over seven into roars of laughter. They can see almost at once that such a long name is bound to get the hero into trouble. On the other hand a six-year-old will see nothing comical about his name drowning the boy in the end. For that age the story is a tragedy. The listener, to find a situation funny, needs to be able to recognize incongruity — as the storyteller, to be success-ful, needs to recognize the tastes of her audience. And this leads us to our concluding word.

A Final Episode — Which Might Be Expanded

We have just dreamed that a popular magazine digest wished to make a condensation of this book. Finding itself embarrassed by lack of space, it was forced to compress the ten chapters into the following:

> For the artist storyteller in religious education two rules compass the spirit, if not the text, of this book. One is

> Know Your Audience

and the other is

> Know Your Story.

" Is this true? " " No, but there is something true about it."

APPENDIX – STORIES FOR TELLING

Unless otherwise indicated, the stories in the Appendix were first published in *Children's Religion*, The Pilgrim Press, and are used by permission of authors and publisher.

THE STILL, SMALL VOICE

Adapted from a story by Shelda R. M. Taylor
(Referred to in chapters VI and X)

ONCE AN OLD man was climbing a mountain. His name was Elijah, and he was a very wise old man. But today he had a problem for which even he, with all his wisdom, could not seem to find an answer.

For many years Elijah had been a sort of leader of his people. They called him a prophet, and a " man of God," as if God and he were special friends. For years the people had looked to him to teach them, and show them what to do, and keep them out of trouble.

But Elijah was discouraged. The people seemed to be growing away from him, and not caring about his teachings any more. They were quarreling and taking sides against each other. Many were listening to a wicked queen who had come from a land where people had careless habits and were untruthful and unfair.

And Elijah was getting old. Before he died he must find another wise leader to teach and guide the people. But where should he find him? He was very troubled.

Now when Elijah was troubled he found that it helped him to go off by himself to think things over. So he was climbing up a high mountain to a cave he knew, to think about his people, and how he could help them; how he could find a new leader for them.

At last he reached the top. He sat down in the mouth of the cave, overlooking a deep valley, and he thought, " Perhaps God will give me some kind of sign to show me what to do." And as he stayed on the mountain top, in the shadow of the cave, he saw a terrible wind sweep down the valley, and he thought, " This may be a sign from God, teaching me what to do."

As he watched, the wind roared through the valley. Tall trees were pulled up by their roots and whirled down the hillside. Huge boulders of rock were torn loose and went rolling down, crashing into a thousand pieces. Clouds of dust filled the air, and he could hear nothing but the sound of the rushing wind. But the terrible wind did not teach him how to help his people.

So Elijah stayed on the mountain top, watching and waiting. By and by the earth began to tremble, and he realized it was the beginning of an earthquake, and he thought, " Perhaps now God will give me a sign." The earth rose and fell; it cracked wide open with a deafening noise, and whole rocks were swallowed up. There was a sound of rumbling and crashing in the valley. But the earthquake did not teach him how to help his people.

Elijah stayed longer on the mountain top, watching and waiting. By and by he saw a fire sweep down the valley, and he thought, " Surely now God is going to give me a sign." He watched the crackling flames as they scorched the grass to blackness, and then went roaring and leaping higher and higher, burning to ashes the trees still standing after the wind and the earthquake had passed. Smoke and flames filled the valley, and when they were gone there was left a charred and blackened hillside. But the fire did not teach him how to help his people.

Then there was a great silence. Elijah came out and stood in front of the cave. He forgot to look for a sign, and he began to think and wonder about his people. He thought for a long, long time. He was very quiet as he thought. By and by he seemed to hear a still, small voice saying, "A *few* of the people are learning good ways, and they can teach the others. There are two good men, Hazael and Jehu, who are strong enough and brave enough to be rulers. And there is that young man, Elisha, who thinks a great deal about the good of the people. He is unselfish enough to want to help them, even now, whenever he can. Elisha also seems a friend of God. He is becoming wiser all the time. *Choose Elisha as the people's prophet.*"

Then Elijah knew he had found an answer to his problem. God *had* given him a sign. It was not in the rush of the wind, nor in the crash of the earthquake, nor in the roar of the fire. Wisdom had come to him when he was very quiet; as he thought, and wondered, and listened to the still, small voice.

BE STILL . . . AND KNOW THAT I AM GOD

Harriet W. Marr
(Referred to in chapters VII and X)

D AVID WAS HURRYING home from school as fast as his feet would carry him. At the cross roads he stopped suddenly, looked toward home, and then turned down the other road away from the village. "I'll go out to the farm, to Grandfather," he thought. Grandfather! The very name was comforting. Grandfather was so gentle, and quiet. Sometimes in talking to David he used the "thee" and "thou" of his own Quaker youth. Grandfather! How David loved and trusted him! Surely Grandfather would be able to help.

So David trudged the long mile out of the village to Grandfather's farm. Grandfather was just coming in from the hay field. He looked keenly at the tired boy. "Thee is in trouble, David," said he. "Come with me. We will walk in the pasture, and thee shall tell me all thy doubts and fears."

Hand in hand they climbed the pasture hill back of the house, and stumblingly David told his story. The war! The awful stories he had heard in current events at school. Why should such terrible things be? Why did God allow it? And then the most terrifying question of all — was there a God? One of the big boys at school had laughed at him, and said there was none.

Grandfather's clasp on David's hand grew firmer and stronger, and his strength seemed to help David without words.

"Let us sit down," said Grandfather. So they sat down on the warm rocks on the hilltop and watched the sun drop below the horizon. The sunset colors flooded the western sky with glory. Grandfather was watching the sunset, but he said nothing. Slowly the glory faded, until the sky was a pale, far-off blue. And still Grandfather was silent. The pale blue grew darker. The velvety night sky arched above them. One by one, the stars came out. And Grandfather had not spoken. The silence grew deeper. Then suddenly David was aware of a Presence, greater, more encompassing, and more comforting even than Grandfather's presence. Once David started to speak, but the silence was too wonderful to be broken. Peace and assurance came in that silence.

The sleepy chirp of a bird broke the quiet, and David turned to Grandfather. "I know now," he said. "I learned it in the silence. I know there is a God. I know things will come out all right finally."

And out of the age-old poetry of the Psalms Grandfather answered him:

Be still, and know that I am God.
God is our refuge and strength,
A very present help in trouble.
Therefore will not we fear,
Though the earth do change,
And though the mountains be shaken into the midst of the seas;
Though the waters thereof roar and be troubled,
Though the mountains tremble with the swelling thereof.
Come, behold the works of the Lord.
He maketh wars to cease unto the end of the earth;
He breaketh the bow and cutteth the spear in sunder;
He burneth the chariots in the fire.
Be still, and know that I am God.

THE CONSTANT STAR [1]

Alice Geer Kelsey

(Referred to in chapters I and X)

OF COURSE, PAVLOS should not have forgotten for one small minute that he was a goatherd. It was especially important that he prove himself trustworthy because his widowed mother depended on the little money he earned tending the flocks of his Turkish neighbor, Zia Effendi. He should have kept his eyes on the goats every minute of every day — but just once he forgot.

It had been a long time since he had eaten his lunch of hard dark bread and cheese and followed the goats under a wild apple tree, bowed down with ripe, red fruit. Every boy knows that the apples at the top of a tree seem sweetest. Up the tree went Pavlos. Apple after apple he munched. He swung his legs contentedly, and just for a moment completely forgot that he was a goatherd.

" Oh, the goats! " Pavlos remembered with a start. He slid down the tree, making a new tear for his patient mother to patch. " Where are they? "

Not a goat was in sight!

Pavlos ran wildly over the hills, calling. He stood still, holding his breath, to listen. Not a switch of a woolly tail! Not the tinkle of a little brass bell!

" They must have gone home by themselves! " Pavlos looked at the glow where the sun had just slipped behind the mountains. " It's after the time we usually start. They ought to know the way home by this time."

Pavlos ran down the hilly trail toward the village. Each time that he rounded a boulder or mounted a hilltop to gain a new view of the trail in the gathering dusk, he hoped for the sight of his flock. " They must be beyond the next rise of ground," he would say as he ran on.

" They must be in their own fold," he said when he reached the last hilltop above his village. It was almost dark now, but the white of the goats would have been visible, had they been on the path. " I hope Zia Effendi will not be cross that they come alone."

But Zia Effendi was cross — not because the goats had come home alone, but because they had not come home at all.

" They must be here," said Pavlos. " They were nowhere on the hills. I would have heard their bells tinkling even if I could not see them."

" Back to the hills, young man, and find those goats! " ordered Zia Effendi.

[1] From *Stories for Junior Worship* by Alice Geer Kelsey. Copyright 1941 Whitmore & Stone. By permission of Abingdon-Cokesbury Press.

"It is dark." Pavlos shivered as he gazed at the hills rising so blackly. "Let me go for them in the morning. It is warm tonight. They will be all right."

"All right alone on those hills? " Zia Effendi laughed mockingly. "Do you hear that noise? "

Pavlos heard and shivered. It was the howl of a jackal far off on the hillside.

Zia Effendi began telling what the jackals would do to a flock of defenseless goats. Pavlos could not help thinking what these same jackals would do to one small boy.

"Go back to the hills and find those goats! " There was no arguing with Zia Effendi when he spoke like that.

Suddenly Pavlos felt an arm about him.

"I wish I could go with you," it was his mother's voice, "but the little brother is sick. I cannot leave him. Here is bread and cheese to eat on the way. Keep saying the prayer, 'Our Father,' that we say in church every Sunday. The Father will keep you safe."

Pavlos took the bread, gave his mother a hug, and started off into the blackness. It was so much darker going away from the lights of the little home village! Only the stars were with him — and the jackals.

He had heard the jackals howl at night when he played with the village boys, but he had never realized before how threatening were their voices. His legs felt as limp as the macaroni cooked in his mother's big copper kettle. On he went, stumbling over rocks and brambles. Round and round the hilltop he wandered. He had lost all sense of direction. All he knew was that somewhere on the hills were the goats, and that he must find them before the jackals did. He tried to hush his own wheezing breath so that he could hear the tinkle of a little brass bell, if one of the goats should stir. They must be asleep now, sleeping so soundly that there would be no tinkling. He realized now that they had probably gone to sleep before he had given up his hunting for them. The sound that never ceased was the howling of the jackals. The voices seemed to come from every side. They seemed to be closing in on him.

"It is growing late." Pavlos talked out loud to give himself the feeling of companionship. "I can tell from the position of the Great Dipper. It is not where it is in early evening."

Pavlos tried to remember the prayer his mother had told him to say, but his mind was so numb with fear and weariness that the words would not come. Nor would any other words of comfort.

He stumbled over a rock and sat where he fell — too tired and dis-couraged to wander further. Suddenly, just over a big rock from him, came the sweetest sound he had ever heard — the tinkle of a little brass bell. Feeling his way carefully, he rounded the rock and found the sleeping goats huddled close together. One of them was scratching his ear with his hind leg, making that blessed tinkle.

Pavlos threw himself in the middle of the flock, patting the goats, counting them, crying tears of relief into their warm silky coats.

"Every goat is here! " cried Pavlos.

The jackals on the hillside howled, but they did not seem so near nor so terrifying now that Pavlos was no longer alone.

"Wake up, my good goats! " called Pavlos. "We must go home."

The goats staggered sleepily to their feet and stood about Pavlos, waiting to be led. The boy turned slowly round and round. On every side was blackness. The lights of his home village lay hidden behind some of the hills. But in which direction? He looked this way and that way, but the darkness seemed alike on all sides. He knew that the village was north of the hills where he was standing. But which way was north? The night was growing late. He could tell by the way the Great Dipper had swung along its nightly journey about Polaris, the North Star.

"The North Star! " Pavlos fairly shouted this name to the black hills and the drowsy goats and the howling jackals. "The North Star never seems to move. It will lead me home. It is always in the north."

Pavlos gathered the goats about him and followed the star, the "constant star that guides men by its light." It was hard walking and slow, but not for one moment did Pavlos feel lost. The planets might take their wandering paths among the stars and the constellations might take their nightly swing about the North Star, but the one fixed star guided him home.

At last the few lights still burning in the village came into view. As Pavlos gave a last look at the guiding star, the words of the prayer his mother had urged him to say flashed back into his mind, "Our Father which art in heaven . . . for thine is the kingdom, and the power, and the glory forever. . . ."

Pavlos, gazing up at the stars, added a prayer of his own: "Our Father, who made the stars obey your laws, I thank you."

THE SECOND MILE[1]

Truman B. Douglass

(Referred to in chapters VIII and X)

THE GREAT ROAD that stretched for miles in both directions was crowded. Groups of people on foot traveled steadily onward. Donkeys, heavy-burdened, passed along. A long train of camels with great bulky loads high on their backs plodded by. The boy David, standing by the side of the road, watched everything with eager eyes.

"Someday I'll follow the road on and on and on," he thought. "I'll follow it down to the Great Sea — and I'll not stop even there! "

His eyes fell upon a single figure, walking alone along the crowded road. "He's a Roman soldier," thought David. "I can tell by the way he's dressed. How I hate the Romans! If it weren't for them we Jews would be free again. Then we shouldn't have to pay their taxes! Or obey their laws! I hate them all! "

He stared at the Roman soldier who was almost opposite him now in the road. Suddenly the soldier stopped. He shifted the heavy pack he carried and eased it down to the ground. Then he straightened up again and stood resting a moment, watching the people passing by.

David still stared at him, thinking angry thoughts. Then just as the soldier turned to pick up his pack once more he noticed David standing not far off.

"Here, boy," he called. "Come here! "

David wanted to turn and run but he did not dare. No one dared to disobey one of the soldiers of Rome. David went nearer, slowly. The soldier motioned to his pack. "You will carry it for me," he said.

Now David knew well that there was no help for it. He knew the hated Roman law. Any Roman soldier could make any Jewish boy or man carry his load for him in any direction he was traveling, for one mile.

"But only for one mile! " thought David, angrily, as he picked up the pack.

The soldier had already turned away and started on along the road. He did not even bother to look back to see that David was following him. He knew he would not dare do anything else.

David followed. The pack was heavy but David was strong. He swung along easily but his thoughts were angry. He wanted to throw the soldier's pack down in the dirt and stamp on it. He wanted to shout and rage at that hated Roman soldier striding ahead of him. But he could do nothing except follow along, keeping his bitter thoughts to himself.

[1] Adapted by Florence M. Taylor.

122

"Well, it's only a mile," he thought, "just one mile. He can't make me go a step farther. Only one mile."

The words made a sort of song in his mind in time to his steps. "One — mile; one — mile."

Then as he was plodding along David suddenly remembered another day when he had walked along this same road. He had gone out a little way from the city with some of his friends to find a young teacher of whom they had heard. They had found him out on the hillside among a crowd of people. David had stopped with the others to listen to what he said.

"What made me think of him now?" wondered David with one part of his mind. Another part was still repeating over and over, "one — mile; one — mile."

"Of course," he remembered suddenly. "The Master used those very words. What was it he said about one mile?" He walked on, frowning, for a moment before he could remember. Then he said the words to himself. "'Whosoever shall compel thee to go one mile, go with him two.' That was what he said!" David had not paid very much attention to it at the time. He remembered now other things the Master had said. "'Love your enemies.' 'Do good to them that hate you.'" Then once more David found himself repeating the strangest of them all. "'Whosoever shall compel thee to go one mile, go with him two.' Does he mean — could he mean — like — now?" David puzzled. "But why? Why should I go more than one mile?"

David was so busy thinking that he did not notice that the soldier had stopped, and so he almost ran into him.

"You have come a mile," said the soldier. "Give me the pack."

"I will go on," said David. And he did not know why he said it. "It has not seemed far. I am not tired."

The Roman stared at him in surprise, and for the first time David really looked into his face. He saw that the soldier was very young. He saw too that he was very, very tired, in spite of the straight, soldierly way in which he stood.

"You have come a long way," said David.

"Yes," said the other, "a weary way of many miles."

"Have you far to go?"

"I go to Rome."

"So far!" said David. "Then let me carry your pack another mile. There is no one here to take it. Another mile will be nothing."

"You are very kind," said the soldier, and his face was still full of surprise.

So they went on, only now the Roman waited for David and walked beside him along the road. And suddenly David found himself talking to the soldier as if they had known each other for a long time. He told him all about his home and family. He listened while the soldier talked of his travels in far places. They were so busy talking that the distance seemed short.

"Tell me," said the soldier at last, "how did it happen that you offered to come this second mile?"

David hesitated. "I hardly know," he said. "It must have been something the Master said, I think." Then he told the soldier all that had happened out on the hill and all that he could remember of the Master's teachings.

"Strange!" said the soldier thoughtfully. "'Love your enemies.' That is hard teaching. I should like to know this Master."

They had come now to the top of a hill and to the end of the second mile. David looked back along the road toward his home. "I must go back," he said.

The soldier took his pack and shouldered it again. The two clasped hands. "Good-by . . . friend," said the soldier.

"Good-by . . . friend," answered David, smiling up into the soldier's eyes.

As David strode back along the road the words of the Master kept running through his mind: "'Whosoever shall compel you to go one mile, go with him two.'" And as he repeated the words he found himself adding with a strange, deep joy: "It works! There's something in it! I walked one mile behind an enemy — I walked the second mile and found a friend!"

"THAT NOVO"[1]

Jeanette Perkins Brown
(Referred to in Chapter I)

ONCE A CHILD had to leave his own home and come to a new part of the world to live. He brought with him his box of treasures, his paints and crayons, a knife, and some small animals he had whittled out of wood, and even some shapeless chunks of wood in which he could imagine more little carved animals.

The child had had a frightening time in his old home. It had made him shy with strangers, and with everybody but his mother he stuttered a little. But she knew how bright he was, and how many things he could do. "You will learn quickly the ways and speech of Americans," she told him. "They will be glad of all you can bring them. America is made up of people who have come from other lands who bring their gifts and ideas to her."

So the child went to school in his new home and began to learn. The other children called him Novo because his own name was too long and hard for them. But they did not know what good ideas he had for them, for at the first mistakes he made in trying to speak their language – they laughed.

It made him feel stupid, and after that he was afraid to speak. Whenever he tried, he stuttered so badly the children would not wait to hear what he had to say. On the playground they would point at him and say, "That Novo!" That made him feel queer and so he kept out of their way.

Each day when his mother would ask, "What did you learn in school?" he would tell her all the new words he had learned, but when she asked, "What did you do in school today?" he would answer, "Nothing."

One day he came home humming a tune. "It's an American song," he explained.

"Did you sing it in school?" his mother asked.

"The others did," he answered. "But they didn't think I could, and my voice wouldn't come out."

"Why not?" his mother asked. "You can sing now." So he could, but singing to his mother was different. She knew that of course he could sing.

Another day after school he got out his paints and started to paint a big picture on paper which he spread out on the floor. "It's a nice picture," his mother said, watching him. "Did you paint in school today?"

"The others did," he admitted. "But they don't think I can paint."

[1] Written for the Department of Race Relations, The Federal Council of the Churches of Christ in America, and reprinted by special permission.

"Why not?" asked his mother. "You can paint now." So he could, now. When he had finished, his mother liked his picture so well she hung it on the wall.

On a third day he told his mother that some of the children had been working in clay. "I can make squirrels and rabbits, can't I, Mother?" he asked, taking from his pockets some of the figures he had whittled from wood. "Of course you can," she said. "Did you make some in school?" "No," he said, "I never had worked in clay, and they didn't think I could make the shapes." "Why not?" asked his mother. "You make them in wood, and that is harder. But how will the others ever know what you can do unless you show them?" Novo thought about that.

Novo was still thinking about it when he got ready for school next morning. He put in his pocket some of the little wooden animals he had carved. He even told his mother he would like to take his picture with him and she helped him roll it up. But on the way he kept wondering if the other children would care about what he could do. Suppose they should laugh at him and say, "That Novo!" The lonely, frightened feeling came back.

It had taken him so long to make himself ready today that he found school already had begun. He took off his coat and hat, in the cloak-room, and stood still, wishing he need not go in before his class. Voices came to him clearly. The door was open. The class was making plans for a Fair. The frightened stuttering feeling suddenly grew worse, for he heard the words he dreaded most of all. "That Novo," a child was saying, "he can't do anything." Novo was so still he hardly breathed. He heard Miss Meylink, the teacher, say, "Everybody can do something."

"Well, then, why doesn't he show he can?" a child asked, and the teacher answered, "We haven't made Novo feel he belongs yet. The minute he does you'll see what he can do. I often think," Miss Meylink went on, "that he must feel as my father did when he came to this country as a little boy." Novo was listening hard now. Miss Meylink's father had come to this country as a little boy! Then her family had come from another land, just as Novo and his mother had! He was glad he had learned so much English, for he could understand now.

"My father has often told me," she was saying, "how like an outsider he felt. He could speak no English, and he wore long full trousers, which were tight around the ankles. He even wore wooden shoes, which the other children thought very funny. But they did not laugh at him long, for he and his Dutch father, my grandfather, had a great deal to give to this country. They built a great dairy farm, and showed other farmers a new way to bring water to their farm lands which my people had learned in the old country. And when my father grew up he loved his new country so much he started a school to train boys to be better farmers here. Yet, when he first came, the other children thought he couldn't do anything."

Miss Meylink stopped. "That's just what we said about Novo," said a voice that was Marion's. Everything was quiet for a moment. Then a voice that was Joseph's said, "That was like my father, too. He told me he was only eight years old when he came to America, and he couldn't make out what people were saying, so all the children thought he was dumb. He said it made him act even dumber, just trying to talk to them. He said he wanted to go back where people could understand him. But it's a good thing for America that people like him come here and stay, because now he works in a laboratory and discovers things that help everybody to keep well. Say, do you s'pose we make Novo feel dumb?"

Novo hardly heard that question. He was too surprised to find that Joseph's family, too, had once belonged to another country. Did everybody come from somewhere else, he wondered. Then he remembered what his mother had told him a long time before: "America is made up of people from other lands who bring their gifts and ideas to her." Slowly he walked through the cloak-room door.

"Here's Novo now," the boy named Joseph said, jumping up and going toward him, and the girl named Marion who sat next to him said excitedly, "We're going to have a Fair, Novo, an 'All-Nations Fair.' And we're going to show how all kinds of people help to make America interesting because everybody brings something different that he can do. What can you do, Novo, that will be like a present from your country? Oh, dear," she stopped again. "I forgot, you can't understand." "I do understand," said Novo quite clearly — and everybody was surprised because he did not stutter — "I can paint." He unrolled the big picture. "Why, Novo!" the children said, "we didn't know you could paint! Could you paint a big one for the back of our Fair?"

"Yes, I could," said Novo, again without stuttering. All his confidence was coming back now, and he pulled from his pocket a chubby bear, a rabbit, a squirrel and a kitten. "I can make animals, too, with my knife," he said happily. "We shall have many for the Fair, a whole forest full, yes? Your clay ones and my wooden ones, and sell them for the Red Cross?" The children were delighted.

"Oh, Novo, what good ideas you have!" Charles said, and when Mary added, "Isn't it lucky that you came here, Novo, you can do so much!" he knew that never again would he have that lonely, frightened feeling here. He "belonged" now.

JANEK'S PROBLEM [1]

Ruth Hunt Gefvert
(Referred to in Chapter I)

J ANEK [Janek — Yah'nek] lay very still on his half of the narrow bed. Beside him his brother Stan slept soundly.

"Why shouldn't he sleep well?" thought Janek, bitterly. "He has no sore places on his arms and legs to burn and itch and keep him awake." Sometimes it helped to blow gently on his arms or to wave them above the covers of the bed; the cool air seemed to ease the hurting. But tonight Janek tried to be quiet. Sometimes he disturbed Stan, and the older brother would waken and be angry with him.

Usually Stan was good-natured and patient but more and more often lately he was short-tempered and cross. It made Janek sad to think about it, for he and Stan had always been good friends as well as brothers. There was another reason, too, why Janek wanted to keep on good terms with him. Stan was in charge of the school garden. American school friends had sent seeds to their village and the garden now was half-grown. The schoolmaster had gone away for two weeks and left Stan, the oldest and most dependable student, in charge of caring for the garden.

"Be sure the plants are well-watered," he had said, "and that weeds and worms and insects do not invade our garden." Everyone in the school knew how important these things were, for it had been a long time since there had been good vegetable seeds in the village, and they were planning to make the most of these. Some of the vegetables would go into stews and soups so all the students could have the good of them. A few of the best vegetables would be saved for seeds for another year.

Everyone had helped to dig the ground and plant and tend the seeds and all the students did their part in making the garden a success. But yesterday Stan had told Janek sternly that those who didn't do their part would get no vegetables. Janek wasn't sure whether Stan really meant it or not, and he didn't know whether the schoolmaster had told him to say it or if Stan had made it up just to scare Janek. It was true that Janek had not helped very much lately. It hurt so terribly to bend over to pick bugs and pull weeds, and the sore places on his hands made even closing his hands painful. But Janek was not one to complain, so he had made no excuses for not working hard in the garden. Janek had pretended not to hear, but Stan's words worried him just the same. If only he could think of something that he could do in the garden that would really help!

So Janek tried not to think of this worry, nor of his hurting arms and legs. Instead he began to think again about the house. This was his favorite thought. He began in his mind, remembering the time when they

[1] From *Newsletter for Boys and Girls* by Ruth Hunt Gefvert. Used by special permission of the author and the American Friends Service Committee.

had lived in the root-cellar after the war. Even now he could feel the dampness and dark cold of that underground room where they had been so crowded together. Then he remembered how they had gathered up bricks and tiles from the rubble and begun to clean the old mortar off. That had been the hardest job and it had taken more than a year for all of them working together — his father and mother and Stan and himself — to get enough tiles and bricks for a new home.

But at last there had been enough. Janek's father and a skilled neighbor had begun putting up the walls of the little house. And finally it was finished.

"It is not so big nor so handsome as our old house," his father had said, "but it is a home that will shelter us through all weather." And then he and his mother and the two boys had bowed their heads while their father said a prayer of thanksgiving to God for their new home. Janek was sure that in all Poland no family had been as thankful as his, nor any boy as proud and happy as he.

Afterwards there had been dancing and merrymaking by all the neighbors in celebration. Janek could not remember so much laughing and joking and fun since the war had come and gone from his country.

Remembering all this, Janek felt better. It was not hard now to lie still beside his sleeping brother. Drowsily he listened to all the soft animal sounds coming from the next room. How glad he was they had followed the old custom and built the stable as part of the house. Dreamily he heard the quiet muttering of the hens, the warm snuffling sound of the cow, a contented grunt from one of the pigs. Listening to all these warm, comforting, friendly sounds, Janek fell asleep.

But when morning came, Janek could scarcely get up, so sore were his arms and legs, and now even his back hurt. He looked so sick that Stan was frightened and called his mother.

"Thank goodness," she said, after she had looked at the sore places on her young son's body, "this is clinic day and there will be a doctor in the village. I will take him there and see what they can do for him."

In a small voice Janek said, looking up at his brother, "I may not be able to come to the garden today. I hope. . . ."

Stan smiled and patted Janek's shoulder. "Don't worry, fellow, I'll do your share today."

"But I want to help," Janek insisted. "I have been trying and trying to think of something I can do to help, only it does hurt so to. . . ."

"Forget it," said Stan. "We'll find you a job you can do easily until you are well again."

But Janek continued to worry. He tried hard to think of how he could help in the garden in spite of his sore arms and legs. "There must be something," he thought.

The doctor had put some soothing medicine on Janek's sores, and bandaged his arms and legs and his waist. Then he said to Janek's mother,

"Pani [Pani — pah'nee — means Madam], there is really little I can do for this boy. The medicine will help to heal the ulcers, but they may come back. You see, Janek's body needs certain vitamins and minerals. The lack of them affects some people this way. There are many children in Poland and in other parts of Europe who have this same trouble. Others it affects differently. Some children grow thin and very tired. Sometimes it makes them nervous, irritable, and cross."

"Maybe," thought Janek, "maybe that is why Stan has been so bad-natured lately. I must remember when he gets cross with me again."

His mother asked the doctor, "How can we get the vitamins and minerals the children need?"

The doctor looked thoughtful for a minute before he answered. "One source," he said, "is good red meat, cheese, butter. And even more, in this case, fresh green vegetables. But I realize how scarce these things are, and how expensive they are even when one can find them."

"We will have vegetables," Janek announced loudly and proudly. And then he wished he hadn't, for he remembered that he had done very little work in the garden and he shouldn't boast. The doctor was pleased, though, when Janek explained about the seeds from America and the good garden that was growing from them.

The doctor smiled. "That is fine, Janek. The vegetables will be a real medicine for all of the children in the village, as well as good eating. I hope you will put some weight on, young man; you are as thin as a scarecrow."

Janek blinked and looked hard at the doctor. That was it! Afterwards he could not remember thanking the doctor or leaving the clinic or hurrying as fast as he could to the garden next to the school. When the garden was in sight and all the other children busy hoeing, pulling weeds and carrying water, he shouted, "I've go it! I've got it!"

All of them looked at him strangely. Stan asked, "What have you got, Janek?"

Janek was so excited and out of breath he could scarcely tell them. "I have a job to do in the garden," he said. "After you have finished working here in the morning you all have other things to do and so you have to leave the garden."

"I know," said one of the others, "and that is when the mischievous crows get in all their bad work. But what has that got to do with you, Janek?" he asked.

"Even though I cannot do the work here that you do," he answered, "I can wave my arms and shout and scare the crows away. I can stay here all afternoon every day and watch for them," he told them, hoping they would think this was an important enough job.

Everyone agreed that it was very important. Stan was proud of his brother and his eyes twinkled wickedly. "My little brother will be our official scarecrow," he said.

NATHAN'S FRIEND
Myra D. Auten
(Referred to in chapters I and X)

THE LITTLE VILLAGE where Nathan lived was right at the edge of the country of Galilee. There were hills all around the village. To the north, friendly Galilean hills; to the west, hills that looked down on the sparkling ocean; to the east, hills that sloped toward the Jordan River; and to the south — oh, to the south the hills were like a stout wall to keep away the Samaritans.

Nathan had never seen a Samaritan, but he had heard about them. Sometimes he heard the men of his village talking together.

"It was a Samaritan all right who stole that donkey," he would hear them say. Or, "When we saw that big rock rolled onto the road, we knew the Samaritans were up to their tricks again." Or, when a boy was really misbehaving, "He acts just like a Samaritan," the men would say.

And the village women talked too. "As cruel as a Samaritan," "as ugly as a Samaritan," "as stupid as a Samaritan."

Many tales were told of the wicked ways of Samaritans. It was no wonder Nathan and the other village children shivered when Samaritans were mentioned.

But though Nathan shivered, he also wondered, and his wondering was greater than his fear. Today he had made up his mind. He would climb the steep and rocky hill road to the south and look for a Samaritan!

Of course he did not expect the Samaritan to see him! He could run quite fast, and he planned to be very careful when he came to the top of the hill which led into Samaritan Land.

He said to his mother, "I am going into the hills. May I have a little lunch to take? I'll be home early. May I go?"

His mother lifted a fresh loaf of bread from the oven carefully. The little brown loaf was round and flat. It looked very good. Nathan watched his mother put it on the table beside five other loaves just like it.

When it was in the row his mother said, "I think you may go. There's a nice trail to the east. Climb to the top of the hill and see if there are boats on the river. Or you could go north where the shepherds take their sheep. Perhaps that would be better. Only do not go too far, and be sure to be back by sundown. I will give you a lunch and you may share it with a friend."

Nathan's mother wrapped two little loaves of bread and a handful of dates in a square cloth. She tied the ends of the cloth together. Nathan tucked the bundle into his wide, soft belt.

"I'm going by myself," he said. "I'll eat all the lunch myself."

Mother laughed and patted his shoulder. "But if you should find a friend to go with you," she said, "you'd like to have enough to share. Be home early."

Nathan hurried away. He felt a little troubled. Mother had said east or north and he was going south. Mother had said he might see the river or the shepherds, but he was going to try to see — a Samaritan! At any rate Mother had said nothing about not going toward the south.

The path was steep. The sun was very hot, and there were many rocks in the way. Nathan began to grow tired. He came to a very big rock which stood exactly in the middle of the path. In fact, the path seemed to stop at the foot of the rock.

"If I could climb up on top of this rock," Nathan thought to himself, "I'd be so high I could surely see into the Samaritans' country. If I were on top of such a big rock, no Samaritan could get at me. I could look all I wanted to. No one would ever know I was there."

It was such a good idea that he began to scramble up the rock, finding little uneven places to help him and getting along better than he had supposed he would. So he came to the top. The rock was high above the path where he had climbed, but on the other side it sloped easily down to the ground. This surprised him. He waited a minute to catch his breath and look around, and it was then he heard the little whistle. He turned to where the sound had come from and saw a boy about his own size blowing on a wooden whistle and watching him.

The boy stopped blowing the whistle when he saw that Nathan had seen him and called, "Hello. Come help me look for our donkey. He's pulled his tie rope loose and strayed away. He's always doing that."

Nathan ran down the sloping rock to his new friend. "Our donkey does that, too," he said. "As soon as he's loose he goes straight to the thistle patch. Then I get stuck with thistles when I go to bring him home."

"Donkeys are all alike, I guess. That's just the way ours does," said the boy. They walked along together.

Each of them was looking for the missing beast. Nathan saw something move among the bushes. It was a gray donkey.

"There he is, over there. See! " he cried, and began running to where the donkey was eating thistles.

The other boy ran, too. The donkey lifted his head and saw them coming. Then he ran!

The donkey ran easily among the rocks and bushes, and the boys followed, shouting and laughing. It was like a game. Then, as if he had had a long enough chase, the donkey stopped and waited for the boys to come near enough to snatch up the tie rope.

"I'll tie him to that big rock," said the boy. "You help me lift it up so we can put the rope around. He'll not get away from this one."

The rock was heavy, but working together, they managed to fasten the end of the rope around it. The donkey began to eat again, as calmly as if he had never even thought of running away, and the two boys sat down to rest and to watch him.

"My name is Nathan; what's yours? " Nathan asked.

"I'm Jared," the boy told him. "I'm glad you came along just when you did — I'd have been chasing him yet. My, I'm hungry. It always makes me hungry to chase that donkey. Look, I've some bread and cheese for my lunch. You have some with me."

"I've bread and dates," said Nathan. "We'll put our food together and have a feast."

So they spread their food on Nathan's cloth, and ate. "This cheese is good," said Nathan. "My mother says she can always tell cheese from Galilee. It's better than any other."

Jared looked up quickly. "Galilee! Why does she say that? I never hear of any good thing coming from Galilee. Why, it's the Galileans who always steal our donkeys, and throw rocks at people."

"Steal donkeys! Why, we do not. It's the Samaritans who steal donkeys, and they're the ones who throw rocks, too. Anybody knows that," said Nathan.

"But — why — but —" stammered Jared. "Aren't you a Samaritan? I thought you must be. You're so friendly, and you helped me get the donkey. You look just like anybody. If you aren't a Samaritan, why are you here in Samaria? "

"In Samaria! " said Nathan, looking around fearfully. "I didn't know I was! I didn't mean to be. I just wanted to see what a Samaritan looks like. I've heard about them, back in our village —"

Then he stopped and looked at Jared, and Jared looked at him. And then both of them began to laugh together.

"Isn't it silly? " said Jared. "Why, the men of our village say all Galileans carry stones in their belts to throw at us Samaritans; that all Galileans steal donkeys. You haven't any stones, and you helped me find my donkey. You're just like me! "

Nathan nodded. "You know what, Jared," he said. "We're boys, but we know more than the men in both our villages."

"The men in my village would forbid me even to talk to you," said Jared, "and I like you the best of any boy I know. I can't even ask you to come home with me! Oh, Nathan! "

"I couldn't go even if you asked me," Nathan said. "Promise me, you'll never believe again that all Galileans are bad."

"I promise," said Jared solemnly. "But you must believe there are good Samaritans, too."

"I do believe," said Nathan simply.

The boys stood quietly together. The shadows had grown longer. The donkey who had been eating lifted his head and shook his ears, and turned to look at his young master.

"We must go," said Jared. "Will you come again, Nathan? "

"I'll try," said Nathan. "Thank you for the cheese. Good-by, friend."

"Good-by, friend," answered Jared. "I'll watch for you."

Nathan scrambled down the rock. He could no longer see Jared, but he heard him call, "Good-by, friend." Nathan walked steadily on toward home.

"Well, Nathan, did you see anything interesting?" his mother asked when he was at home again.

"I saw a Samaritan," said Nathan.

"A Samaritan! Did he hurt you? Where was he? Stealing something, I'll be bound. We'll tell your father," said Nathan's mother.

"No, no," said Nathan. "We played together. He gave me some cheese. I helped him find his donkey. He's a boy, just like me. His name is Jared, and I want to see him again some day."

"A boy like you," Mother said slowly. "I've always heard — but then perhaps the children are different. Sometimes, I've wondered what Samaritans were really like, and whether they were all as bad as we've been told.

"They're folks," Nathan nodded his head. "Just folks like us."

Mother turned back to where she was fixing supper. "Who knows?" she said. "Maybe some day when you are grown up —"

Nathan fidgeted. "Why wait to grow up?" he wondered. He and Jared had a head start. They did not have to wait to grow up. They were friends already.

THE LITTLE BOY WITH A BIG STICK

Jeanette Perkins Brown

(Referred to in Chapter I)

Tony was a very little boy, but he always carried a very big stick. He was a very little boy, but he wore a very big scowl. To look at him you would have thought a small black thunder-cloud was approaching, and you probably would have got out of his way when you saw that big stick.

Tony had carried that big stick ever since he came to live in the city. He was only five and couldn't go to the school where the children went who were just a little older. That does not mean that he was not learning something every day. Oh, no. Tony was learning many things and everything he learned was making Tony into a certain kind of little boy.

The very first day he learned that the big boys on his block would knock him down and take away his apple or his cookie if they happened to want to. That is why he carried a big stick. He had learned that the stick made other boys and girls afraid of him.

If you had asked Tony what he knew about big boys he would have told you, "Big boys are mean." That is what he had learned from the boys on his block. It made him into the little black thunder-cloud he seemed to be. He scowled whenever he saw any boys at all, or even any other children, whether they had been unfriendly to him or not. He waved his big stick and scowled, and the little children would scream and run away and say, "He's a bad boy!"

When he heard that, he scowled all the more. Nobody likes to be called a bad boy. He got a bigger stick.

One day a teacher from a Neighborhood House in the next street discovered Tony. She was carrying a box full of little baskets filled with earth. In the earth in each basket was a pansy plant.

She saw Tony sitting on the curb. "Hello," she said, "what's your name?" She thought she knew all the children on that block. Tony scowled, and held up his stick. He tried to scare her. He never thought for a minute that here might be a friend. One of the things he had learned since he had come to this city was that it was an unfriendly place. He started to wave the stick. Then he saw the pansies. He had no idea what they were. He had never seen a pansy. He still scowled, but he put down his stick.

Two children came running down the street shouting, "Teacher! Teacher!" When they saw Tony they stopped and pointed at him. "Don't speak to him, Teacher," they said; "he's a bad boy."

Tony's scowl was blacker than ever, but his eyes opened a little wider when he heard the teacher say, "Of course he's not a bad boy."

She walked toward Tony. He was so little that the scowl and the stick seemed bigger than he, but he did not look funny to the teacher. He looked sad.

Tony was looking at the pansy plants. "Would you like one?" the teacher asked. Tony put out a finger and touched a petal, ever so carefully. "Smell it," the teacher said, inviting him, "it smells good." Tony put his nose close to one of the flowers and drew a deep breath. Then he gently felt the pansy again. The teacher watched. Was the scowl going? The children watched, too. He didn't really seem "bad" now.

"What's your name?" the teacher asked again; "do you live here? Shall I take the flower into your house?"

Tony jumped up. He still carried his stick, but the scowl was going. He opened the door and led the way down a hall to another door. No one was at home.

"See," she said, taking from her box a basket with a big pansy blooming and some smaller buds, "this is for you. Take care of it. Every day give it some water to drink, like this." She poured some water from a pitcher on the table. "Tomorrow," she said, "I'll come to see you again." Tony watched her solemnly. He did not smile, but he did not scowl quite so blackly. He still held on to his stick.

The next day when the teacher came down the street there were two girls and two boys with her. "I'm going to see that little new boy I saw yesterday," she was telling them. "Do you know his name?"

"Yeah, that boy with the stick that scowls; he's Tony," a child said. "He's bad."

"No, he's just unhappy. Something has hurt him, deep down inside. If he had some friends, he'd smile," the teacher said.

"Naw," the children answered, "he never did smile yet!"

Then they saw Tony. He was standing in the doorway. The basket with the pansy plant was in his hand. He looked as if he were waiting for someone. He never even noticed the children, but when he saw the teacher he said "Hi!" He was very solemn, but he was not scowling, and he did not lift his stick. The teacher looked at the plant, and saw that it had been watered.

"You took good care of it, Tony," she approved. "Tony, wouldn't you like to come with the other children over to the playground? You may swing and teeter and climb, and I'll bring you back, or one of the boys will." Tony looked uncertainly at the others, then put one hand in the teacher's. The other held on to his stick, while his arm hugged the plant.

They walked a block to the playground on the corner, and suddenly one of the boys who had said, "He's bad," had an idea. "Maybe I can make him smile," he whispered to the teacher. "Here, Tony, want a swing? I'll help you!" Again Tony looked a little fearful, but the boy was holding out his hand. One little girl held his plant, another held his stick, while Tony held on with both hands to the ropes. The bigger boy pulled the seat back, and pushed again.

As the swing shot forward everybody who was watching had a sudden surprise. Tony was laughing! The scowl was gone entirely, and he was actually squealing, "Again! Do it again! "

" He's laughing! " cried the girl who was holding his plant.

" He doesn't look bad any more! " said the girl who was holding his stick.

" He isn't afraid any more," said the teacher, going into the Neighborhood House.

"Again! Do it again! " the little boy in the swing squealed.

The big boy laughed — the big boy who had had the idea.

" O-kay," he said, and pushed again.

THANK OFFERINGS

A Story Talk by *Margaret Dulles Edwards*
(Referred to in Chapter VIII)

D ID YOU EVER stop to think how we got the stories about Jesus that we have in the New Testament? It is a long story. We haven't time to tell it all today, but one little verse helps show us the way these stories were first collected.

Now the verse is this: " Remember the words of the Lord Jesus, how he said: It is more blessed to give than to receive." (Acts 20: 35) Perhaps you have often said or heard that verse without thinking what an interesting story it has to tell. It tells the story of the beginning of our records about Jesus. For you know Jesus did not write down anything himself, and so far as we know, his friends did not write down anything while he was alive.

After Jesus' death the people that had known and loved him got together and talked about him. One would say, " Do you remember the words of Jesus, how he said . . ." and then another, " Do you remember what Jesus said —" and each would tell the story or saying that he remembered best.

Years passed by, these friends of Jesus grew old. Many of them died, and the younger people as they grew up realized that soon there would be no one left who could say: " I remember." There was danger that his words might be forgotten. Perhaps it was then that the grown-up children in these younger generations began to put in writing the stories and sayings the older people had told them. In this way little collections grew up in different towns and cities, some alike, some different, and years later others who realized how important these records were put them together in larger collections, so today we have the four collections of stories and sayings of Jesus which we call " The Gospels."

Whenever we hear the verse, " Remember the words of the Lord Jesus, how he said: It is more blessed to give than to receive," or, " To give is happier than to get," as the verse is given in another translation, we can imagine a group of Jesus' friends talking together about him. Perhaps when someone said this, others in the group were reminded especially of the stories and sayings of Jesus about giving. Perhaps someone said, " Do you remember the day Jesus was in the temple? He sat over against the Treasury " (read Mark 12: 41-44); and when he had finished another said: " Do you remember that Jesus said: If you bring your gift " — (read Matthew 5: 23, 24).

So we have these and many other stories and sayings of Jesus.

Let us go back in our thoughts to the time when Jesus was living and one of these incidents took place. Let us imagine ourselves with him in the great city of Jerusalem. It is at the time of one of the religious feasts or holidays when Jews from all over the world came to the temple with their offerings. Every Jew looked forward to attending at least one of these festivals each year. They were joyous occasions, and Jesus, as a faithful Jew, was often one of the pilgrims in the crowd that passed through the narrow city streets and went up to the temple. This temple was a magnificent building with its great open courts surrounded by colonnades of pillars and its steps leading from one court to another till one came to the inner Holy of Holies, symbol of the presence of God himself.

As Jesus came into the temple, perhaps he passed through the outer court rather quickly. It was noisy there with the bleating of lambs, the cooing of frightened doves kept on sale for offerings, and the loud voices of the money-changers who exchanged foreign coins for the temple shekels.

Across the court he hurried, up the steps, and through the gate called Beautiful. Perhaps he paused for a moment by this gateway to look up at its magnificent doors of Grecian brass, doors so heavy that it took the efforts of twenty men to open them each morning and close them again at night. He liked their strength.

Now he was in the Court of the Women, so called not because it was especially for women, but because women were not allowed to go any farther into the temple. One side of this court was known as the Treasury. Here against the wall stood thirteen money chests. They were a strange shape, like great trumpets turned upside down, the large part at the base, the small part at the top; and over each a label telling for what the money dropped in would be used.

Jesus sat down near these treasury boxes. Sooner or later every pilgrim would come by, for it was a law that every Jew should bring to the temple each year a half-shekel in tribute.

What a procession it was, for here came Jews, not only from different parts of Palestine, but Jews from all over the world.

There was a Persian Jew, who had come the long route from beyond the Euphrates River on camel back; an Egyptian Jew, who probably rode north on his sturdy little donkey. The Jews from Greece and Rome had come in sailing ships across the Mediterranean Sea and the journey across the seas had taken them many weeks.

Jesus watched them as they passed through the portico, paused before the boxes, read the labels, and dropped in their coins: some of the boxes were marked for " Temple Tribute," " Incense," " Gold Dishes," " Wood." Others were marked for " Free-Will Offerings." Jesus knew that the money dropped in the " Free-Will " boxes was sometimes given as an expression of thanks. Perhaps a mother was happy that a little baby had come to her home; a husband was thankful that his wife had recovered from a severe fever; or sometimes the money was given to help some wish come true; a landowner was eager to sell his vineyard for a good price, a merchant longed for the safe return of a rich cargo; a mother had sent her son into the army — she hoped no harm would come to him. Or the money was dropped in so that the giver would receive special credit for being generous and stand well in the estimation of the priests.

As Jesus watched these givers he was reminded of the days when he was a boy at home. How hard they all used to work to save a few coins for the " Free-Will " box! There were always so many payments demanded by law: first, the heavy taxes claimed by the Roman government, then the gifts required of every faithful Jew — a tenth of everything to be taken each week to the town meeting house, the one-half shekel to be taken each year to Jerusalem — and after that, how could they save another mite?

It was while these thoughts were going through Jesus' mind that he was startled by the sound of a trumpet. He looked up, and saw approaching the treasury a rich and important-looking man. His servant preceded him, blowing a trumpet to make sure that no one would touch his master — also that all would notice him. He was dressed in splendid robes of silk and fine linen. He walked with a sure firm step. He held his head high, looking about to make sure he was seen. Then with a lordly gesture, he drew a gold coin from his belt, held it high, and dropped it in the chest so that it fell with a loud clanging noise. He was feeling especially pleased with himself today. Business had gone well. He knew how to manage. Among other things he had engaged a forlorn-looking widow to work in his kitchen. She was too poor and too afraid to ask for much pay, so he had engaged her for two mites a day — only a cent in our money; yes, indeed, he knew how to succeed. Today he could easily afford to drop a gold piece in the " Free-Will " box. This would bring him great credit.

Not far behind him crept this same poor widow. She crouched low and walked quietly, hoping she would pass unnoticed in the crowd. Her dress was patched and darned. She looked so shabby! She was so poor, she had so little to give — it was hard for a widow to get any help. She had been out of work for so long, but at last she had earned something. To be sure it wasn't much, only two mites for working from sunrise to sunset, but what little she had she would bring to the temple to show her gratitude. Quickly and quietly she slipped her two mites into the box. It was the whole of her day's earnings. Then as silently she was gone, lost in the crowd, unnoticed.

Unnoticed, yes, yet not by everyone. For Jesus saw this strangely different pair who had come to the temple, each with his gift. He did not know either one of them, and yet perhaps he did know all that was important. Turning to the friends who were with him, he said, " Did you see that poor widow? She has cast more in than all the others who have put their money into the Treasury. They have put in their surplus, but she has given out of her need."

THE LEGEND OF THE BLACK MADONNA[1]

Margaret T. Applegarth

(Referred to in Chapter IV)

A MAGNIFICENT CHURCH was being built in a certain city and there was need for one great stained glass window to go in a certain conspicuous wall. The committee in charge felt that it would be wise to have artists from all over the world submit designs for this window, and so they issued a general notice about their requirements, and set a date when all sketches would be due. Many famous painters entered drawings in the contest, but the one design on which all the committee agreed unanimously was made by an artist of unknown name and fame. The committee wrote to him enthusiastically that they could not imagine any design which could better fill their requirements for the Church of the Redeemer than his sketch entitled, " The Place Where the Young Child Lay." It was exactly what they wanted, and they commissioned him forthwith to go ahead with the work, the details of which they entrusted to him, warning him to have all in readiness for the dedication of the church on Christmas Eve.

The Unknown Artist was naturally very much elated at this fine opportunity to win fame and money, and also he saw in it a chance to work out a certain grudge which he had had against all mankind — a grudge so deep and bitter that he thought of it day and night, and kept himself secluded in his attic studio rather than try to mix with people whom he hated. He took the sketch of which the committee approved so enthusiastically, and he made certain little changes here and there with almost wicked delight, then he called in his wife and baby that they might pose for the enlarged painting which he must make.

His wife had just come in from hanging out the family washing and she was wearing a shawl over her head and carrying the baby in the clothes basket. She put down the basket, and leaned over it; then, looking up, said gently, " The baby is sound asleep. If I pick him up he'll awaken and cry. . . ."

" Don't pick him up, stay just as you are; it's perfect, simply perfect. Imagine that the clothes basket is a manger, that you are Mary, the mother of Jesus, and you have leaned over to see if he is sleeping, but now you look up because you hear someone coming. Some people outside on camels; the three wise men . . . and way up here at the top of the canvas I'll paint the star that came and stood over the place where the young child lay . . . stay perfectly still, don't move . . . don't move, dear, it's perfect."

So the painter's wife kept the pose he thought was perfect, and with quick, sure strokes he painted her as she knelt there. And it was a far lovelier picture than he had planned to make, because in the heart of

[1] From *And So He Made Mothers* by Margaret T. Applegarth. Harper & Brothers. Used by permission of author and publisher.

his wife there was none of the bitter grudge that was in his heart. When she looked down at her child, a great peace stole over her and when she glanced up at her husband painting so rapidly and eagerly, a great contentment came over her that at last his great talent had been discovered and the fame deserved was to come to him. Then, too, as she knelt there in that quiet room she began to realize who it was that she represented . . . Mary, the mother of Jesus! What a wonderful thing to feel that in the life of your little sleeping baby the hopes of the whole world were centered! She fell to wishing that her boy could grow up with hands that would comfort the sick and sorrowing. . . . And as she brooded over the wonders of childhood, and determined to train her son in every Christlike attitude, there came over her sweet, tired face a radiance and beauty that was quite different from any look that had ever been there before. The Artist gasped with surprise, catching the rare charm of her expression and painting her in hushed delight. Yet, all the time, underneath his delight, the same old bitter hatred was working, and he kept saying to himself with fiendish glee, " The lovelier I make this picture, the better I can pay them back for all these years of insults and injustice."

Day after day the posing continued, until finally his masterpiece was done, ready for the stained-glass workers; and here his difficulty lay, for if they discovered his secret, everything was lost. Then he thought of a plan, a clever, secret plan that could not help but work. The week before Christmas the various parts of the window arrived in that distant city where the new Church of the Redeemer was already completed. Trained workers began assembling the bits of glass and putting them in place, when a strange oversight bewildered them.

Neither face nor arms of the Madonna and Child could be found high nor low. The workers were frantic until the Artist arrived and calmed their fears by telling them that he had brought the missing parts of the window himself. It was just a whim of his, he said, to put in the faces and arms himself after all the other work was done. When they discovered that he had beyond doubt mastered the art of setting the pieces together, they gladly granted his request. To be sure it was not at all the usual way to put up a window, but after all, the success of this one was his special concern, for it would be his dream come true. And so they went away and left him. He walked into the Church of the Redeemer and looked about him. The whole building was fragrant with holly and pine. The florists who had been busily decorating pulpit, pillars, and pews had long since departed and the Artist was left alone. With set lips and grim determination he climbed the ladders and set to work putting in place the lovely, brooding face of the Madonna, her tender, protecting arms reaching out over the sleeping child. Furiously he worked on into the night until every last piece was in its proper place. Then he climbed down from the ladder and stood back to look at his work with a malicious kind of satisfaction. " Now," he said, " now, I have paid back the world for its treatment of me. I've given these so-called Christians something to think about. They'll not like it, but at least they'll have a new idea. And I shall be more famous than they ever dreamed." And he went out into the twilight of Christmas Eve.

There was the cheerful sound of sleighbells and the bustling of many people doing the last-minute things that always have to be done on Christmas Eve. There were men carrying home sleds and hobby-horses and dolls, there were women carrying home baskets full of good things for the Christmas dinner and little children skipping by with mysterious parcels. "All right," thought the Artist, " go on in your smug, satisfied way; I have a Christmas present for you, too, one you won't soon forget."

When the time arrived for the dedication of the church, he slipped into a back pew, the unknown Artist. And just as he had expected the entire congregation were looking up at his window with startled and disapproving glances. There was whispering . . . nudging . . . and often an angry gesture.

The dedication service went on as planned, the last carol was sung and the Benediction was pronounced, but the congregation stayed on; they stood in the aisles all looking toward the window. " The face of that Madonna is certainly black," said one. " She is a Negro," said another. " Even the child looks like a Negro baby; where is that Artist anyhow? Certainly the glass factory would never make an error like this. The original sketch was not like this. There's foul play somewhere. Why, we can't permit such a thing as this in a magnificent church like ours." All over the church one could hear the protests. "Awful," " Horrible," " Disgraceful," "A black Madonna in a church like this."

And all this time the Artist, hiding behind a pillar, chuckled with glee. " Paying you back; I'm paying you back, you fine white Christians you, all you superior, lordly beings; I'm paying you back, I say, for all the years of insults you've heaped on my Negro head. Horrible of me, was it, to make your Christ Child black, and disgraceful? Not half so horrible and disgraceful as what you fine folks have done to me and yes, to all my people. Shocked, are you? Well, go on being shocked! This is only the beginning! "

The midnight chimes rang out, but that congregation had left the church with anything but good will in their hearts. News of the marred window was telephoned all over the town, and although the early Christmas morning service was usually attended by only a few faithful souls, this year the nave was filled to overflowing, for everybody had come to see the black Madonna. Everyone except the Minister, who was a just and gentle and loving man. All night long he had lain awake wondering, wondering how he was ever going to preach the sermon from the text he had announced. A text that was inscribed in the famous window. " In Him was Life, and the Life was the Light of Men." His whole sermon was built around the window. He had pictured himself pointing to the Christ Child and telling how the hopes of all mankind had once clustered around the place where the Child lay. But how point to a black Madonna and Child as the hope of all mankind? Seven o'clock found him walking into the church packed with a curious, bitter crowd of people whose eyes were turned in one direction. "This settles it," said the Minister to himself. "And, Oh Lord, God, help me to find the words." And he arose and announced his text. "In Him was Life, and the Life was the Light of Men." The congregation were reading those very words in the glass of the window, and some of them were resenting such words under such a picture, when suddenly the morning sun came blazing forth with all the extra dazzle of a snowy winter's day, and as its beams came through the stained glass of the window, a gasp of sheer surprise spread through the church, for in that blaze of sunlight the Madonna's face was shining, pure as an angel's, and the Christ Child was a sheen of dazzling glory. " In Him was Life," repeated the Minister, " and the Life was the Light of Men," and inspired by the transfigured Madonna and Child, he preached a sermon that marked a milestone in the life of every person present.

"Who are you and I that we do not want a black Madonna in our church? In that great day of beginnings when the Lord God made man, did he specify 'let us make white men in our image?' No — let us make man! And to some were given black skins, to some yellow, to some brown and to some white. He must have seen but little difference in these external colors when there are an Africa with over a hundred million black-skinned people, and a China with four hundred million yellow men, and an India with three hundred million brown men, and a Europe and an America with several hundred million white men. So in deep humility this Christmas Day, I ask you, when God looked down last night into this Church of the Redeemer, who really looked black to his all-seeing eyes? That black Madonna? Or you and I with black consternation in our hearts because we demanded that a Madonna must have flesh the color of our flesh? The conceit of us, the curious blackness of our hearts that cannot see the God shine through those of another color. Lift your eyes to the wonderful face of that black mother — the love and tenderness that is there. Like Mary of old she seems to keep all things in her heart and ponder them there. Have you forgotten that the mother of the Christ Child was not a white-skinned woman but an olive-skinned Jew? We need to remember that, my friends. Let us then this morning be wise men and bring our gifts to a Saviour of all mankind. For in Him was Life, and the Life was the Light of men . . . black men . . . and white men."

As the Minister concluded his sermon, a stillness rested over the church that was broken only by the sound of faltering footsteps as a black man came slowly down the center aisle and faced the congregation. "I am the Artist who designed your window, and it was I who fashioned the

Madonna and Child of black glass. It was no mistake of the workers, be sure of that. I did it because I wanted to hurt you to repay you for the way you and your people have hurt me. I wanted revenge, but I got only shame. Something has happened here in this church today to show me that I am as color blind as I thought any one of you. I set out to prove to you what hypocrites you Christians were, and that there was nothing in your religion; but I was wrong, and when God's sunlight shone through that window I knew it. It was a sort of miracle to me and I knew that in the sight of God there is neither black nor white, if his light shines through. I've wronged you insanely and selfishly. I ask you to forgive me. I have here the white pieces of glass that were originally meant for your Madonna and tomorrow I will change them," and the Artist turned to go when a member of the congregation arose and spoke as if for all present. " We'll leave the black Madonna in its place forever, so that all may see how the light that came to earth with the Christ Child is indeed the Light of the World, shining through the faces of God's family regardless of the color of the flesh." The congregation rose as one man, and who can ever tell how far-reaching may be the influence of the black Madonna. Surely that congregation felt it, and as they sang a Christmas hymn together, there was in it the quality of a prayer.

> " How silently, how silently,
>   The wond'rous gift is given!
>   So God imparts to human hearts
>   The blessings of his heaven.
>   No ear may hear his coming,
>   But in this world of sin,
>   Where meek souls will receive him, still
>   The dear Christ enters in."

THE HEAVENLY MUSIC

Die Himmlische Musik

Translated from the German by Jeanette Perkins Brown
(Referred to in Chapter X)

L ONG AGO, in the Golden Age, when the angels played with the peasant
children in their sand piles, the doors of heaven stood wide open, and
the golden, heavenly splendor poured down upon them like rain on the
earth. The people could look from the earth into the open heavens, and
could see the happy heavenly beings walking among the stars. The people
on the earth could call out greetings to the " Blessed " and the Blessed
could answer them. But the most beautiful thing was the wonderful
music which came forth from heaven at that time. God had written the
notes for it himself, and a thousand angels played it with violins and
kettledrums and trumpets.

When the music sounded, all the earth became quiet. The wind ceased
its roaring, and the water in the sea and in the streams stood still. But the
people nodded to each other, and secretly clasped their hands. They felt
strange emotions, such as cannot be described nowadays to a poor human
heart at all.

So it was at one time, but it did not last long. For one day God as a
punishment shut the doors of heaven and said to the angels, " Stop your
music, for I am sad."

Then the angels became sad likewise, and each one sat upon a cloud
with his sheet of music. With their little golden shears they cut the
sheets into tiny pieces, and let them fall down to the earth below. Here
the wind took them, blew them like snowflakes over mountain and
valley, and scattered them over all the world.

And the peasant children seized each a shred, one a large piece, another
a small one, and carefully treasured them. Each bit was very precious,
for it was a part of the heavenly music which had sounded so wonderful.

In time they began to dispute and quarrel because each one imagined
that he had seized the best piece, and at last each one declared that what
he had was the only true heavenly music, and that what the others
possessed was useless fraud, and but the appearance of the real thing.

Those who wished to be very clever — and there were many of these
— made on their piece, at the beginning and the end, a great flourish,
and were particularly conceited about it.

One whistled A and the other sang B; one played in a minor, the other
in a major key; no one could understand the others. In short, it was a
tumult such as one hears in a village school.

So it is today.

But when the last day shall come, when the stars fall upon the earth,
and the sun into the sea, and the people crowd each other at the doors of

heaven, like children for the Christmas tree when the door is thrown open, then will God let the angels gather together again all the bits of paper from his heavenly music book, the small ones as well as the large, and even the very small ones, on which stood only a single note. The angels will fit the pieces together again, and then the doors will fly wide open and the heavenly music will sound forth anew, as beautiful as before.

Then will the children of men stand and listen, wondering and ashamed, and one shall say to the others, " That was your note; — I had that one! " But for the first time again it will sound wonderful and glorious, and quite different, now that all the notes are together and in the right order.

Yes, that's the way it will be, you can depend on it.

TO YOUR GOOD HEALTH [1]

Andrew Lang
(Referred to in Chapter I)

LONG, LONG AGO there lived a king who was such a mighty monarch that whenever he sneezed everyone in the whole country had to say " To your good health! " Everyone said it except the shepherd with the bright, blue eyes, and he would not say it.

The king heard of this and was very angry, and sent for the shepherd to appear before him.

The shepherd came and stood before the throne, where the king sat looking very grand and powerful. But however grand or powerful he might be, the shepherd did not feel a bit afraid of him.

" Say at once, ' To my good health! ' " cried the king.

" To my good health! " replied the shepherd.

" To mine — to mine, you rascal, you vagabond! " stormed the king.

" To mine, to mine, Your Majesty," was the answer.

" But to mine — to my own," roared the king and beat on his breast in a rage.

" Well, yes; to mine, of course, to my own "; cried the shepherd and gently tapped his breast.

The king was beside himself with fury and did not know what to do, when the Lord Chamberlain interfered:

" Say at once — say this very moment: ' To your health, Your Majesty.' For if you don't say it you'll lose your life," whispered he.

" No, I won't say it till I get the princess for my wife," was the shepherd's answer.

Now the princess was sitting on a little throne beside the king, her father, and she looked as sweet and lovely as a little golden dove. When she heard what the shepherd said she could not help laughing, for there is no denying that this young shepherd pleased her very much. Indeed he pleased her better than any king's son she had yet seen.

But the king was not as pleasant as his daughter, and gave orders to throw the shepherd into the white bear's pit. The guards led him away and thrust him into the pit with the white bear, who had eaten nothing for two days and was very hungry.

The door of the pit was hardly closed when the bear rushed at the shepherd; but when it saw his eyes it was so frightened it was ready to eat itself. It shrank away into a corner and gazed at him from there and, in spite of being so famished, did not dare to touch him but sucked its own paws from sheer hunger. The shepherd felt that if he once took his eyes

[1] From *Russische Mährchen* in the *Crimson Fairy Book,* collected and edited by Andrew Lang. Copyright 1903, 1947, by Longmans, Green and Co. Used by permission.

off the beast he was a dead man, and in order to keep himself awake he made songs and sang them, and so the night went by.

Next morning the Lord Chamberlain came, expecting to see the shepherd's bones, and he was amazed to find him alive and well. He led him to the king who fell into a furious passion and said:

"Well, you have learned what it is to be very near death; now will you say, 'To my good health'?"

But the shepherd answered, "I am not afraid of ten deaths! I will only say it if I may have the princess for my wife."

"Then go to your death," cried the king, and ordered him to be thrown into the den with the wild boars.

The wild boars had not been fed for a week and, when the shepherd was thrust into their den, they rushed at him to tear him to pieces. But the shepherd took a little flute out of the sleeve of his jacket and began to play a merry tune, on which the wild boars first of all shrank shyly away; then got up on their hind legs and danced gaily.

The shepherd would have given anything to be able to laugh, they looked so funny, but he dared not stop playing, for he knew well enough that the moment he stopped they would fall upon him and tear him to pieces. His eyes were of no use to him here, for he could not have stared ten wild boars in the face at once. So he kept on playing and the wild boars danced very slowly, as if in a minuet, then by degrees he played faster and faster till they could hardly twist and turn quickly enough and ended by all falling over each other in a heap, quite exhausted and out of breath.

Then the shepherd ventured to laugh at last. He laughed so long and so loud that when the Lord Chamberlain came early in the morning, expecting to find only his bones, the tears were still running down his cheeks from laughter.

As soon as the king was dressed the shepherd was again brought before him. But he was more angry than ever to think the wild boars had not torn the man to bits, and he said:

"Well, you have learned how it feels to be near ten deaths, now say, 'To my good health!'"

But the shepherd broke in with, "I do not fear a hundred deaths! I will only say it if I may have the princess for my wife."

"Then go to a hundred deaths!" roared the king, and ordered the shepherd to be thrown down the deep vault of scythes.

The guards dragged him away to a dark dungeon, in the middle of which was a deep well with sharp scythes all round it. At the bottom of the well was a little light by which one could see if anyone thrown in had fallen to the bottom.

When the shepherd was dragged to the dungeon he begged the guards to leave him alone a little while that he might look down into the pit of scythes. Perhaps he might after all make up his mind to say, "To your good health" to the king.

So the guards left him alone and he stuck up his long stick near the well, hung his cloak round the stick and put his hat on the top. He also hung his knapsack up inside the cloak so that it might seem to have somebody within it. When this was done he called out to the guards and said that he had considered the matter but, after all, he could not make up his mind to say what the king wished.

The guards came in, threw the hat and cloak, knapsack and stick, all down the well together, watched to see how they put out the light at the bottom and came away, thinking that now there really was an end of the shepherd. But he had hidden in a dark corner and was laughing to himself all the time.

Quite early next morning came the Lord Chamberlain, carrying a lamp, and he nearly fell backward with surprise when he saw the shepherd alive and well. He brought him to the king, whose fury was greater than ever, but who cried:

"Well, now that you have been near a hundred deaths, will you say, 'To your good health'?"

But the shepherd only gave the same answer. "I won't say it till the princess is my wife."

"Perhaps after all you may do it for less," said the king, who saw that there was no chance of making away with the shepherd, and he ordered the state coach to be made ready. Then he had the shepherd get in with him and sit beside him, and ordered the coachman to drive to the silver wood. When they reached it he said:

"Do you see this wood? Well, if you will say, 'To your good health,' I will give it to you."

The shepherd turned hot and cold by turns, but he still persisted. "I will not say it till the princess is my wife."

The king was much vexed; he drove farther on till they came to a splendid castle, all of gold, and then he said:

"Do you see this golden castle? Well, I will give you that too, the silver wood and the golden castle, if only you will say that one thing to me, 'To your good health.'"

The shepherd gaped and wondered and was quite dazzled, but he still said, "No; I will not say it till I have the princess for my wife."

This time the king was overwhelmed with grief, and gave orders to drive on to the diamond pond, and there he tried once more.

"Do you see this diamond pond? I will give you that too, the silver wood and the golden castle and the diamond pond. You shall have them all — all — if you will but say, 'To your good health!'"

The shepherd had to shut his eyes tight not to be dazzled with the brilliant pond, but still he said, "No, no; I will not say it till I have the princess for my wife."

Then the king saw that all his efforts were useless, and that he might as well give in, so he said, "Well, well, it's all the same to me — I will give you my daughter to wife. But, then, you really and truly must say to me, 'To your good health.'"

"Of course I'll say it; why should I not say it? It stands to reason that I shall say it then."

At this the king was more delighted than anyone could have believed. He made it known all through the country that there were to be great rejoicings, as the princess was going to be married. And everyone rejoiced to think that the princess, who had refused so many royal suitors, should have ended by falling in love with the blue-eyed shepherd.

There was such a wedding as had never been seen. Everyone ate and drank and danced. Even the sick were feasted, and all newborn children had presents given them.

But the greatest merry-making was in the king's palace; there the best bands played and the best food was cooked; a crowd of people sat down to table and all was fun and merry-making.

And when the groomsman, according to custom, brought in the great boar's head on a big dish and placed it before the king to carve and give everyone a share, the savory smell was so strong that the king began to sneeze with all his might.

"To your very good health," cried the shepherd before anyone else. And the king was so delighted that he did not regret having given him his daughter.

In time, when the old king died, the shepherd succeeded him. He made a very good king and never expected his people to wish him well against their wills; but, all the same, everyone did wish him well, for they all loved him.

ANNA AND THE SPECKLED HEN[1]

Ruth Hunt Gefvert
(Referred to in Chapter I)

Anna got off and walked beside her bicycle. Her legs were tired from pedaling even though the ground was flat here. Just walking slowly and pushing her bicycle like this made her heart race. Almost anything at all that she did any more made her tired.

Anna was discouraged, too. Her mother would be disappointed. She might even scold and say that she herself should have gone to the country to bargain for vegetables. Her mother thought she was too young to trust with this weekly errand. But Anna was sure her mother couldn't have done any better. Not even the farmers seemed to have any vegetables left. In fact, there didn't seem to be any vegetables in all of Germany.

To be sure, Herr Krauss had given her a few beets. But that was all. There were enough to make a very little soup.

Suddenly Anna knew she could go no farther. She would have to stop and rest. She laid her bicycle on its side, making sure the beets did not spill out of the basket. Then she lay down in the cool grass. Almost immediately she was asleep.

She dreamed of food. All her dreams were about food lately, it seemed. This time she dreamed of carrots the color of gold, steaming hot in cream and butter. Even in her dream, though, she knew this was foolish, for she could not remember having had either butter or cream. But her mother had told her about them, and in her dream she could almost tell how wonderful they tasted.

Next in her dream there were tomatoes, beautiful red, juicy tomatoes. There was a great pile of them and Anna was just about to eat one when they disappeared. With a start she woke up. She rolled over and sat up. And there, looking her right in the eye, was a speckled hen. They looked at each other — Anna and the hen.

Suddenly Anna realized that the hen was talking. At least she was clucking and making the kind of talk that speckled hens make.

" Why are you staring at me, you silly thing? " asked Anna. "And making all that noise woke me up," she charged.

" Cu-u-u-t . . . c-uu-tt . . ," said the hen, startled at Anna's cross-sounding voice, and she backed away.

It was then that Anna saw the egg! Carefully she picked it up, still warm.

" Oh, you beautiful, beautiful hen," she exclaimed. " I am sorry I was rude to you. Thank you for this lovely egg."

But the speckled hen had walked off and Anna was left alone with the egg. She felt better now, more rested. She must hurry home so she could

[1] From *Newsletter for Boys and Girls* by Ruth Hunt Gefvert. Used by special permission of the author and the American Friends Service Committee.

give the egg to her mother. Perhaps they could have a very small omelet!

Anna took off the kerchief she wore on her head. Carefully she wrapped the egg in it and laid it tenderly in the basket with the beets. Then she got on her bicycle and started up the road.

But an unhappy thought came to her. The egg wasn't really hers. It belonged to the owner of the speckled hen. Anna pedaled more and more slowly.

"No," she told herself furiously, "the egg is mine. The hen laid it right beside me when I was asleep." Anna went on up the road.

"Anyway, I don't know who owns the speckled hen. And even if I did, they would never know I had the egg."

A little white house sat close to the road. "They can't tell a thing," argued Anna with herself. "I've got the egg all covered up." She began to pedal faster and faster.

But her bicycle seemed to go more and more slowly. And when she got to the white house, her legs wouldn't pedal any longer. Very slowly she got off her bicycle and walked up to the house.

"Yes?" asked the young woman who came to the door.

With the dream of the small omelet fading fast, very reluctantly Anna said, "Do . . . do . . . you own a . . . a . . . speckled hen?"

"Why, yes," said the young woman, "we do." Carefully and very slowly Anna unwrapped her scarf from around the egg and handed it to the woman.

"Then this is yours, too," she said.

"Oh, thank you," said the woman. "That speckled hen is always wandering off and laying her eggs in the most unlikely places. She is the last of our hens, and we do need her eggs for our little boy. He is very ill, you see."

Anna started to leave. The young woman looked troubled. "You have been so kind," she said, "I wish I had something to give you for your basket. But there is so little of everything. I . . . I . . . have nothing to give."

"It is all right," said Anna, and climbed on her bicycle again. She was anxious now to get away from the white house and the speckled hen and the wonderful egg.

When she got home Anna told her mother what had happened. She was afraid her mother would scold her for being so late, and for bringing home only a few beets. She might even be cross that she hadn't kept the egg.

But her mother only smoothed Anna's hair and looked at her for a long time, and smiled.

"Then you are not angry with me, mother? You do not think I am too young to go to the country to bargain for vegetables?"

"No, Anna," said her mother. "I am just thinking what a fine daughter I have. And when one is so hungry all the time, only a real grown-up could have made such a hard decision about the egg."

A JAPANESE FOLK TALE

As told by Jeanette Perkins Brown

(Referred to in Chapter X)

THERE WAS ONCE a mother who was so pleased when her first little son was born that she gave him a long and important-sounding name. It was Tiki-tiki-tembo-no-so-rembo-ara-bara-buski-ip-eri-pendo-hyki-pon-pon-nichi-no-meono-don-bianco. The second little son she called Choey.

One day when Tiki-tiki-tembo-no-so-rembo-ara-bara-buski-ip-eri-pendo-hyki-pon-pon-nichi-no-meono-don-bianco and Choey were playing in the garden, Choey fell into the well.

Tiki-tiki-tembo-no-so-rembo-ara-bara-buski-ip-eri-pendo-hyki-pon-pon-nichi-no-meono-don-bianco ran toward the house, calling, "Mother, Mother! Choey's fallen into the well, and I don't know what to do!" But his mother was nowhere to be seen. He ran inside the house, calling again, "Mother, Mother! Choey's fallen into the well, and I don't know what to do!"

But his mother was in the room farthest back in the house, and not until he had gone through every room did he find her. Then he cried again, "Oh, Mother, Mother! Choey's fallen into the well, and I don't know what to do!"

"What!" his mother said, "Choey's fallen into the well? Well, go and find the gardener, and tell him to get a ladder and put it down the well and rescue him."

So he ran to the gardener.

"Gardener, Gardener! Choey's fallen into the well. Come quickly and get a ladder and rescue him!"

But the gardener was deaf. "Hey?" he said.

"Gardener, Gardener! Choey's fallen into the well. Come quickly and get a ladder and rescue him!"

But the gardener was *very* deaf. He put his hand behind his ear, and said, "You'll have to speak a little louder. I'm rather hard of hearing."

"Oh, Gardener, Gardener! Choey's fallen into the well. Come quickly and get a ladder and rescue him!"

"What!" cried the gardener. "Choey's fallen into the well? Well! I'll go and get a ladder and rescue him."

So he went and brought a ladder, and he rescued him.

A few days later the two boys were playing in the garden again, when all at once poor Tiki-tiki-tembo-no-so-rembo-ara-bara-buski-ip-eri-pendo-hyki-pon-pon-nichi-no-meono-don-bianco fell into the well.

Choey ran toward the house, calling, "Mother, Mother, Tiki-tiki-tembo-no-so-rembo-ara-bara-buski-ip-eri-pendo-hyki-pon-pon-nichi-no-meono-don-bianco has fallen into the well, and I don't know what to do." But his mother was nowhere to be seen.

He ran inside the house, calling again, " Mother, Mother! Tiki-tiki-tembo-no-so-rembo-ara-bara-buski-ip-eri-pendo-hyki-pon-pon-nichi-no-meono-don-bianco has fallen into the well, and I don't know what to do! "

But his mother was in the room farthest back in the house, and not until he had gone through all the rooms, just as his brother had a few days before, did he find her. Then he cried again, " Oh, Mother, Mother! Tiki-tiki-tembo-no-so-rembo-ara-bara-buski-ip-eri-pendo-hyki-pon-pon-nichi-no-meono-don-bianco has fallen into the well, and I don't know what to do! "

" What! " his mother said, " Tiki-tiki-tembo-no-so-rembo-ara-bara-buski-ip-eri-pendo-hyki-pon-pon-nichi-no-meono-don-bianco has fallen into the well? Well, go and find the gardener quickly and tell him to get a ladder and put it down the well and rescue him! "

So Choey ran out to the gardener, crying, " Gardener, Gardener, Tiki-tiki-tembo-no-so-rembo-ara-bara-buski-ip-eri-pendo-hyki-pon-pon-nichi-no-meono-don-bianco has fallen into the well. Come quickly and get a ladder and rescue him! "

" Hey? " said the gardener.

" Oh, Gardener, Gardener, Tiki-tiki-tembo-no-so-rembo-ara-bara-buski-ip-eri-pendo-hyki-pon-pon-nichi-no-meono-don-bianco has fallen into the well. Come quickly and get a ladder and rescue him! "

But the gardener still didn't hear a word. He cupped his hand behind his ear and said, " You'll have to speak a little louder. I'm rather hard of hearing."

This time Choey *shouted*, " GARDENER, GARDENER! TIKI-TIKI-TEMBO-NO-SO-REMBO-ARA-BARA-BUSKI-IP-ERI-PENDO-HYKI-PON-PON-NICHI-NO-MEONO-DON-BIANCO HAS FALLEN INTO THE WELL. COME QUICKLY AND GET A LADDER AND RESCUE HIM! "

" What! " exclaimed the gardener, " Tiki-tiki-tembo-no-so-rembo-ara-bara-buski-ip-eri-pendo-hyki-pon-pon-nichi-no-meono-don-bianco has fallen into the well? Well! I'll go and get a ladder and put it down the well and rescue him."

But by the time he had brought the ladder and put it down the well, alas, poor Tiki-tiki-tembo-no-so-rembo-ara-bara-buski-ip-eri-pendo-hyki-pon-pon-nichi-no-meono-don-bianco was drowned.

And from that day to this, mothers have never given their children such long names.

THE APRON-STRING [1]

Laura E. Richards

(A parable for adults; referred to in Chapter II.)

ONCE UPON A TIME a boy played about the house, running by his mother's side; and as he was very little, his mother tied him to the string of her apron.

"Now," she said, "when you stumble, you can pull yourself up by the apron-string, and so you will not fall."

The boy did that, and all went well, and the mother sang at her work.

By and by the boy grew so tall that his head came above the window-sill; and looking through the window, he saw far away green trees waving, and a flowing river that flashed in the sun, and rising above all, blue peaks of mountains.

"Oh, mother," he said, "untie the apron-string and let me go!"

But the mother said, "Not yet, my child! only yesterday you stumbled, and would have fallen but for the apron-string. Wait yet a little, till you are stronger." So the boy waited, and the mother sang at her work.

But one day the boy found the door of the house standing open, for it was spring weather; and he stood on the threshold and looked across the valley, and saw the green trees waving, and the swift-flowing river with the sun flashing on it, and the blue mountains rising beyond; and this time he heard the voice of the river calling, and it said "Come!"

Then the boy started forward, and as he started, the string of the apron broke. "Oh! how weak my mother's apron-string is!" cried the boy; and he ran out into the world, with the broken string hanging beside him.

The mother gathered up the other end of the string and put it in her bosom, and went about her work again; but she sang no more.

The boy ran on and on, rejoicing in his freedom, and in the fresh air and the morning sun. He crossed the valley, and began to climb the foothills among which the river flowed swiftly, among rocks and cliffs. Now it was easy climbing, and again it was steep and craggy, but always he looked upward at the blue peaks beyond, and always the voice of the river was in his ears, saying "Come!"

By and by he came to the brink of a precipice, over which the river dashed in a cataract, sending up clouds of silver spray. The spray filled his eyes, he grew dizzy, stumbled, and fell. But as he fell, something about him caught on a point of rock at the precipice-edge, and held him, so that he hung dangling over the abyss; and when he put up his hand to see what held him, he found that it was the broken string of the apron.

"Oh! how strong my mother's apron-string is!" said the boy: and he drew himself up by it, and went on climbing toward the mountains.

[1] From *The Golden Windows* by Laura E. Richards, by permission of Little, Brown & Co.

BIBLIOGRAPHY

The letters **o.p.** indicate that a book is out of print.

Storytelling

THE WAY OF THE STORYTELLER, Ruth Sawyer. The Viking Press. A great storyteller shares her rich experience and joy in her art, and tells eleven of her best-loved stories. Valuable reading and story lists.

HOW TO TELL STORIES TO CHILDREN, Sara Cone Bryant. Houghton Mifflin Co.

WRITING JUVENILE FICTION, Phyllis A. Whitney. The Writer, Inc.

THE ART OF THE STORY-TELLER, Marie L. Shedlock. Dover Publications, Inc.

STORIES AND STORY TELLING, Edward P. St. John. The Pilgrim Press. o.p.

Pamphlets

STORIES, a list of stories to tell and to read aloud. Compiled by Eulalie Steinmetz. The New York Public Library, New York, N. Y.

STORIES TO TELL TO CHILDREN. Carnegie Library of Pittsburgh (Boys and Girls Department), 4400 Forbes St., Pittsburgh 13, Pa.

STORYTELLING. Association for Childhood Education, 1201 Sixteenth St., N.W., Washington 6, D. C.

FOR THE STORYTELLER. National Recreation Association, 315 Fourth Ave., New York 10, N. Y.

Useful Collections of Stories

THE ANIMALS' CHRISTMAS, poems, carols, and stories chosen by Anne Thaxter Eaton. The Viking Press. Includes " The Holy Night," by Selma Lagerlöf, " The Three Magi," by Lura Belpré, and other stories and legends that remind us of one of the most lovable parts of the Christmas tradition.

ANTHOLOGY OF CHILDREN'S LITERATURE, Edna Johnson, Carrie E. Scott and Evelyn R. Sickels. Second edition. Houghton Mifflin Co. A new edition of an excellent collection of materials for use with children or with teachers of children. Contains a graded reading list and biographical notes.

THE BLUE FLOWER, Henry van Dyke. Charles Scribner's Sons. o.p.

BOYS AND GIRLS AT WORSHIP, Marie Cole Powell. Harper & Bros.

CHILDREN'S STORIES TO READ OR TELL, FOR PLEASURE AND UNDERSTANDING. Edited by Alice I. Hazeltine. Abingdon-Cokesbury Press. Thirty-seven selections chosen with skill and discrimination from both the classics and modern writings.

THE FIRESIDE BOOK OF CHRISTMAS STORIES, edited by Edward Wagenknecht. The Bobbs-Merrill Co., Inc. Includes "The Other Wise Man," by Henry van Dyke; "The Man at the Gate of the World," by W. E. Cule.

FOR THE CHILDREN'S HOUR, Carolyn Sherwin Bailey. The Platt & Munk Co., Inc. Also, STORIES CHILDREN WANT, by the same author.

THE FRIENDLY STORY CARAVAN, compiled and edited by Anna Pettit Broomell. J. B. Lippincott Co. This volume adds a dozen new stories to a selection of the best tales from the author's well-loved books, THE CHILDREN'S STORY GARDEN and THE CHILDREN'S STORY CARAVAN.

FROM LONG AGO AND MANY LANDS, Sophia L. Fahs. The Beacon Press.

GREATNESS PASSING BY, Stories to Tell to Boys and Girls, Hulda Niebuhr. Charles Scribner's Sons.

HERE AND NOW STORY BOOK, Lucy Sprague Mitchell. E. P. Dutton & Co., Inc. Also, ANOTHER HERE AND NOW STORY BOOK, by the same author.

THE LONG CHRISTMAS, Ruth Sawyer. The Viking Press. Thirteen beautiful stories, one for each day of the long Christmas, from Christmas to Epiphany. Some are ancient, some new, some humorous, and all are interspersed with carols and Christmas rhymes.

MISSIONARY HERO STORIES, edited by Nina Millen. Friendship Press. Twenty-eight stories for leaders to tell to boys and girls of junior and junior high age. See also titles in two pamphlet series, "Eagle Series" and "Frontier Series," brief biographies of missionaries and other well-known Christians at home and abroad.

MISSIONARY STORIES TO TELL, a compilation. Friendship Press. Also, MORE MISSIONARY STORIES TO TELL.

THE QUESTING SPIRIT, RELIGION IN THE LITERATURE OF OUR TIME, selected and edited by Halford E. Luccock and Frances Brentano. Coward-McCann, Inc. Includes the reading version of the radio play, "Isaiah and the United Nations," by Stanley H. Silverman.

STORIES FOR JUNIOR WORSHIP, Alice Geer Kelsey. Abingdon-Cokesbury Press. Also, MORE STORIES FOR JUNIOR WORSHIP, by the same author.

STORY AND VERSE FOR CHILDREN, selected and edited by Miriam Blanton Huber. The Macmillan Co. A wide range of materials has been included to present a well-rounded and balanced program of children's reading. Valuable book lists follow each group of selections.

THIRTY STORIES I LIKE TO TELL, Margaret W. Eggleston. Harper & Bros.

WHY THE CHIMES RANG AND OTHER STORIES, Raymond Macdonald Alden. The Bobbs-Merrill Co.

WORSHIP PROGRAMS AND STORIES FOR YOUNG PEOPLE, Alice A. Bays. Abingdon-Cokesbury Press.

Background Books for Bible Stories

THE BIBLE

REVISED STANDARD VERSION. Thomas Nelson & Sons.
AMERICAN STANDARD VERSION. Thomas Nelson & Sons.
KING JAMES VERSION.
THE BIBLE, A NEW TRANSLATION, James Moffatt. Harper & Bros.
THE COMPLETE BIBLE, AN AMERICAN TRANSLATION (with the Apocrypha), J. M. Powis Smith and Edgar J. Goodspeed. University of Chicago Press.
THE NEW TESTAMENT IN MODERN SPEECH, translated by Richard Francis Weymouth. Harper & Bros.

REFERENCE BOOKS

CRUDEN'S COMPLETE CONCORDANCE, Alexander Cruden. Includes references to both the King James and the Revised versions. The John C. Winston Co.
WALKER'S COMPREHENSIVE CONCORDANCE, J. B. R. Walker. Based on the King James Version. The Macmillan Co.
DICTIONARY OF THE BIBLE, edited by James Hastings. Complete in one volume. Charles Scribner's Sons.
ABINGDON BIBLE COMMENTARY, edited by F. C. Eiselen, Edwin Lewis, David G. Downey. Abingdon-Cokesbury Press.
COMMENTARY ON THE HOLY BIBLE, J. R. Dummelow. The Macmillan Co.
PEAKE'S COMMENTARY ON THE BIBLE, edited by Arthur S. Peake. Thomas Nelson & Sons.
A HARMONY OF THE GOSPELS, Wm. Arnold Stevens and Ernest Dewitt Burton. Charles Scribner's Sons.
JESUS IN THE RECORDS, H. B. Sharman. Association Press.
GOSPEL PARALLELS, A SYNOPSIS OF THE FIRST THREE GOSPELS. The text of the Revised Standard Version is used. Thomas Nelson & Sons.
THE STORY OF THE BIBLE, Edgar J. Goodspeed. The University of Chicago Press. For background of the Gospels, see section on New Testament, chapters 8-11 and 17.
HOW TO READ THE BIBLE, Edgar J. Goodspeed. The John C. Winston Co. For brief explanation of authors and purposes of the four Gospels, see pages 1-9 and 19-21.
ENCYCLOPEDIA OF BIBLE LIFE, Madeleine S. and J. Lane Miller. Harper & Bros.
THE BIBLE GUIDE BOOK, Mary Entwistle. Abingdon-Cokesbury Press.
HOW THE EARLY HEBREWS LIVED AND LEARNED, Edna M. Bonser. The Macmillan Co.

THE USE OF THE BIBLE WITH CHILDREN, Ethel L. Smither. Abingdon-Cokesbury Press.

STORY BOOKS

THE BOY JESUS AND HIS COMPANIONS, Rufus M. Jones. (Little Library Series) The Macmillan Co. Stories of the boyhood of Jesus told by the great Quaker leader.

THE DRAMA OF ANCIENT ISRAEL, John W. Flight in collaboration with Sophia L. Fahs. The Beacon Press. This book uses both biblical research and recent archeological findings to present greater perspective on the early background of Israel.

JESUS THE CARPENTER'S SON, Sophia L. Fahs. The Beacon Press. This story biography offers realistic treatment of the " young patriot " growing up in an invaded country. Familiar teachings are related with imagination to actual happenings.

THE LITTLE BOY OF NAZARETH, Edna M. Bonser. Harper & Bros. An imaginative account of the life of Jesus up to twelve years of age. Offers excellent background material for the storyteller.

MOSES, Katherine B. Shippen. Harper & Bros. Miss Shippen has written for young people a biography of Moses in which he emerges as a real, living person.

MOSES: EGYPTIAN PRINCE, NOMAD SHEIKH, LAWGIVER, John W. Flight. The Beacon Press. A dramatic and convincing narrative of an enslaved people led toward nationhood by an unforgettable leader.

THE STORY OF THE BIBLE, Walter Russell Bowie. Abingdon-Cokesbury Press. A useful and basic book of Bible stories, told in a style closely following the Bible text.

Books Referred to in This Book

THE APOSTLE, Sholem Asch. G. P. Putnam's Sons.

BAMBI, Felix Salten. Simon & Schuster.

SUE BARTON, NEIGHBORHOOD NURSE, Helen D. Boylston. Little, Brown & Co. The sixth book in this popular " career " series.

BEDTIME STORY-BOOKS, Thornton W. Burgess. Little, Brown & Co.

BLACK STALLION, Walter Farley. Random House.

BY AN UNKNOWN DISCIPLE, Anonymous. Harper & Bros.

DOCTOR GEORGE WASHINGTON CARVER: SCIENTIST, Shirley Graham and George D. Lipscomb. Julian Messner, Inc.

GEORGE WASHINGTON CARVER: AN AMERICAN BIOGRAPHY, Rackham Holt. Doubleday & Co., Inc.

A CHRISTMAS CAROL, Charles Dickens. Editions published by various publishers, including The Macmillan Co., The John C. Winston Co., Holiday House, E. P. Dutton & Co., Inc., Thomas Y. Crowell Co.

CRIMSON FAIRY BOOK, Andrew Lang. Longmans, Green & Co., Inc.

CRY, THE BELOVED COUNTRY, Alan Paton. Charles Scribner's Sons.

DOCTOR DOLITTLE, THE STORY OF, Hugh Lofting. J. B. Lippincott Co.

EIGHT PRIZE-WINNING ONE-ACT PLAYS, selected by Hugh S. Quecket. Geo. G. Harrap & Co., Ltd., London. Includes "The Flaw," by Cyril Roberts.

THE FIVE CHILDREN AND IT, E. Nesbit. Coward-McCann, Inc. The first of three books of the Magic Tales.

FROM IMMIGRANT TO INVENTOR, Michael Pupin. Charles Scribner's Sons.

GENTLEMAN'S AGREEMENT, Laura Z. Hobson. Simon and Schuster, Inc.

THE GOLDEN WINDOWS, Laura E. Richards. Little, Brown & Co. o.p.

THE GREATEST STORY EVER TOLD, Fulton Oursler. Doubleday & Co., Inc.

"Isaiah and the United Nations," a radio drama by Stanley H. Silverman, in THE QUESTING SPIRIT.

JESUS THE SON OF MAN, Kahlil Gibran. Alfred A. Knopf, Inc.

JOHNNY TREMAIN, Esther Forbes. Illus. by Lynd Ward. Awarded the John Newbery Medal, 1944. Houghton Mifflin Co.

LASSIE COME-HOME, Eric Knight. The John C. Winston Co.

THE LITTLE LOCKSMITH, Katharine B. Hathaway. Coward McCann, Inc.

THE LITTLE PRINCE, Antoine de Saint-Exupéry. Harcourt, Brace and Co.

MY FRIEND FLICKA, Mary O'Hara. J. B. Lippincott Co.

FLORENCE NIGHTINGALE, Jeannette C. Nolan. Julian Messner, Inc.

FLORENCE NIGHTINGALE: THE ANGEL OF THE CRIMEA, Laura E. Richards. Appleton-Century-Crofts, Inc.

NORTH TO THE ORIENT, Anne M. Lindbergh. Harcourt, Brace and Co.

THE OTHER WISE MAN, STORY OF, Henry van Dyke. Harper & Bros.

"Saul," Robert Browning, in Complete Poetical Works. Houghton Mifflin Co. Browning's poems are also published in the World's Classics (Oxford University Press); Everyman's Library Series (E. P. Dutton & Co., Inc.); and by Modern Library, Inc.

TOM SAWYER, ADVENTURES OF, Mark Twain (Samuel L. Clemens). Editions published by Grosset & Dunlap, Harper & Bros., Heritage Press (The George Macy Companies, Inc.), David McKay Co., The John C. Winston Co., The World Pub. Co.

ALBERT SCHWEITZER: GENIUS IN THE JUNGLE, Joseph Gollomb. The Vanguard Press.

STORY-TELL LIB, Annie Trumbull Slosson. Charles Scribner's Sons. o.p.

THE STORY TELLER, Maud Lindsay. Lothrop, Lee & Shepard Co., Inc. o.p. By the same author: STORY GARDEN FOR LITTLE CHILDREN and FUN ON CHILDREN'S STREET (Lothrop); MOTHER STORIES and MORE MOTHER STORIES, published by The Platt & Munk Co., Inc.

WHAT DO YOU THINK? Anna Pettit Broomell. Harper & Bros.

THE YEARLING, Marjorie K. Rawlings. Charles Scribner's Sons. Also published by Modern Library, Inc.

Stories Referred to in This Book
and Books in Which They May Be Found

Cinderella

TOLD UNDER THE GREEN UMBRELLA, Association for Childhood Education, Literature Committee. The Macmillan Co.

BLUE FAIRY BOOK, Andrew Lang. Longmans, Green & Co., Inc.

ALL THE FRENCH FAIRY TALES, Charles Perrault; retold by Louis Untermeyer. Didier Publishers.

TOLD AGAIN, Walter J. de la Mare. Alfred A. Knopf, Inc.

Epaminondas and His Auntie

STORIES TO TELL TO CHILDREN, Sara Cone Bryant. Houghton Mifflin Co.

The Fig Seed

FROM LONG AGO AND MANY LANDS, Sophia L. Fahs. The Beacon Press.

The Gingerbread Man   *Also called*, The Gingerbread Boy

STORIES TO TELL TO CHILDREN, Sara Cone Bryant. Houghton Mifflin Co. Published as separate title by Albert Whitman Co.

Henny-Penny   *Also called*, Chicken Little

ENGLISH FAIRY TALES, Joseph Jacobs. G. P. Putnam's Sons.

ANIMAL STORIES, Walter J. de la Mare. Charles Scribner's Sons.

TALES OF LAUGHTER, K. D. Wiggin and N. A. Smith. Doubleday and Co., Inc.

The Jar of Rosemary

THE STORY TELLER, Maud Lindsay. Lothrop, Lee & Shepard Co., Inc. o.p.

The Juggler of Notre Dame

THE WAY OF THE STORYTELLER, Ruth Sawyer. The Viking Press.

AUCASSIN AND NICOLETTE AND OTHER MEDIEVAL ROMANCES AND LEGENDS, translated from the French by Eugene Mason. (Everyman's Library) E. P. Dutton & Co., Inc.

The Little Engine That Could, Watty Piper. Illus. by Lois L. Lenski. The Platt & Munk Co., Inc.

The Little Red Hen

STORIES TO TELL TO CHILDREN, Sara Cone Bryant. Houghton Mifflin Co.

FOUR-AND-TWENTY BLACKBIRDS, edited by Helen Dean Fish. J. B. Lippincott Co. Published as separate title by H. D. Fish (Nursery Book Series), Houghton Mifflin Co., and (Little Golden Book), Simon and Schuster.

The Lump of Salt

FROM LONG AGO AND MANY LANDS, Sophia L. Fahs. The Beacon Press.

Maisie's First Meeting

THE CHILDREN'S STORY GARDEN, Anna Pettit Broomell. J. B. Lippincott Co.

A Musician and His Trumpet

FROM LONG AGO AND MANY LANDS, Sophia L. Fahs. The Beacon Press.

No Room at the Inn
ONE BASKET, Edna Ferber. Simon and Schuster.
The Old Woman and Her Pig
ENGLISH FAIRY TALES, Joseph Jacobs. G. P. Putnam's Sons.
TOLD UNDER THE GREEN UMBRELLA, Association for Childhood Education, Literature Committee. The Macmillan Co.
MOTHER GOOSE, NURSERY RHYME BOOK, edited by Andrew Lang. Frederick Warne & Co.
HOW TO TELL STORIES TO CHILDREN, Sara Cone Bryant. Houghton Mifflin Co.
Palace Built by Music
WHY THE CHIMES RANG AND OTHER STORIES, Raymond Macdonald Alden. The Bobbs-Merrill Co.
The Promise
THE STORY TELLER, Maud Lindsay. Lothrop, Lee & Shepard Co., Inc. o.p.
Little Red Riding Hood
Edited by Elizabeth Orton Jones. (Little Golden Book) Simon and Schuster.
The Song That Traveled
THE STORY TELLER, Maud Lindsay. Lothrop, Lee & Shepard Co., Inc. o.p.
The Story of the Three Bears *Also called,* Goldilocks
The Story of the Three Little Pigs
Both of these stories are found in:
THE GOLDEN GOOSE BOOK, L. Leslie Brooke. Frederick Warne & Co.
ANIMAL STORIES, Walter J. de la Mare. Charles Scribner's Sons.
ENGLISH FAIRY TALES, Joseph Jacobs. G. P. Putnam's Sons.

INDEX OF STORIES